IN
ENEMY HANDS

A BRITISH TERRITORIAL SOLDIER IN GERMANY
1915-1919

The Rue de Lille, Ypres, in peaceful days before the war.

IN
ENEMY HANDS

A BRITISH TERRITORIAL SOLDIER IN GERMANY
1915-1919

MALCOLM HALL

TEMPUS

First published 2002

PUBLISHED IN THE UNITED KINGDOM BY:
Tempus Publishing Ltd
The Mill, Brimscombe Port
Stroud, Gloucestershire GL5 2QG

PUBLISHED IN THE UNITED STATES OF AMERICA BY:
Tempus Publishing Inc.
2 Cumberland Street
Charleston, SC 29401

British Library Cataloguing in Publication Data.
A catalogue record for this book is available from the British Library.

ISBN 0 7524 2620 6

Typesetting and origination by Tempus Publishing.
PRINTED AND BOUND IN GREAT BRITAIN.

Contents

Note on Place Names

Belgium has long been the joint home of two different races: in the eastern part live the French-speaking Walloons, while the western half of the country, which we know as Flanders and which was the scene of so much of the fighting in the First World War, is the traditional homeland of the Dutch-speaking Flemings. One result of this has been that the names of many of the towns and villages in that region can be found in either of two forms, French or Flemish. Although today's visitor will find that, on maps and road signs, it is the Flemish name which prevails, at the time of the Great War, it was more usually the French version which was used (by the British at any rate, who tended to find the French language rather easier to cope with than the unfamiliar Flemish!). Thus, the town which today is universally called by its proper Flemish name of Ieper was, to the generation which knew its ruins in 1914–1918, never anything but Ypres (except to Tommy Atkins, who, in his own inimitable vernacular, usually referred to it as 'Wipers'). Similarly, Flanders, a name whose resonance to that generation was every bit as strong as that of Ypres itself, is today known to its inhabitants (and they should know!) as Vlaanderen.

However, since it is their French names by which they were known to the British who fought there or who waited at home and which are usually to be found in contemporary English-language accounts as well as in modern writing on the subject, I shall use the same here. Most of the differences are in any case minor and should present no difficulty. There are however just a few, such as the examples already referred to, where the correlation between one language and the other is not so readily distinguishable. Thus, it may be worth pointing out that the town of Roulers is now usually known as Roeselare, while the visitor to what was Courtrai will find himself in Kortrijk and even the French town of Lille is, to the Flemish, Rijsel.

Foreword

One sunny spring morning, a few months after the start of the new millennium, I stood in a narrow, unhedged lane running along a low ridge in Belgium. Just behind me, what had once been the top of the ridge had been removed to form a cutting, through which the A19 motorway now passes, its presence proclaimed by the intermittent roar of passing vehicles. To my front, a mile or two away in the haze of the early spring sunshine, rose the Gothic towers of the Flemish town of Ieper. In the immediate foreground, the land – ploughed, like much of the neighbouring countryside at that time of year – climbed gently upwards towards my feet. Eighty-five years earlier, the town, which had already entered British military legend under its French name of Ypres, had, after nine months of war, been reduced by German shelling to an uninhabited ruin. Exactly eighty-five years before, on 8 May 1915, the remnants of an English Territorial battalion, known as the Rangers, with the ruined town at their backs, had been struggling through German machine gun and artillery fire, with the forlorn task of reaching the low ridge on which I was now standing, to come to the aid of the Welshmen of the 1st Monmouthshires, holding out in their wrecked trenches on the forward slope behind me. Very few, if any, made it that far and by that evening the Rangers, in whose ranks my father was then serving, had virtually ceased to exist. He himself was one of those who found themselves on the wrong side of the front line, prisoners of the enemy. He was undoubtedly one of the lucky ones; while he and many from the other battalions involved that day were being marched off to a long captivity, numbers of their erstwhile comrades lay dead on the gentle south-western slope of the Frezenberg ridge, at which I found myself gazing, on that day many years and two world wars later.

Were he able to return to the area today, I doubt if he would recognise it. First and foremost, the ruined town into which he marched on a February evening of that far-off year has risen from its ashes: over many years, between the two wars and then resuming after the second, its broken stones were steadily reconstituted from their apparently hopeless confusion into their former shapes. In a miracle of human resilience, the handsome buildings of the ancient medieval town, so wantonly destroyed by man's perverse deployment of the gifts of science, have been rebuilt in exactly their old form. The fine Lakenhalle (or Cloth Hall) with its great clock tower once more presides over the wide central square, complemented by the traditional Flemish façades of the subordinate buildings alongside, while behind rises the ornate spire of St Martin's Cathedral. Opposite the Cloth Hall the Rijselsestraat (or Rue de Lille) forms one of the exits from the square, whose buildings too have risen from their once-melancholy wreckage. Less pleasingly, a large part of the square itself, in earlier times the haunt of strollers and a few horse-drawn vehicles, is today one vast, busy car-park, animated by a continual movement of cars and buses. The eastern exit from the square, the Meensestraat, passes through the Menenpoort, or Menin Gate, unveiled in 1927 to commemorate many thousands who died defending the Ypres

Salient, but who have no known grave. Still today, the buglers of the Ypres Fire Service keep faith with those who paid that sacrifice when, each evening at eight o'clock in the course of a short ceremony, they sound the Last Post.

Out on the northern edges of the town, where lines of men – French and Algerian, British and Canadian – once marched up to man the trench lines, he would find that drear industrial sites have sprawled across the former farmland, obliterating the village of La Brique and edging towards the rebuilt St Jean. In the countryside itself, around places like Wieltje and St Julien, apart from the disappearance of the railway line to Roulers and the appearance of the motorway to Courtrai, the scene is more recognisable. The farmers are still busily working the land, as they were then until the conflict bundled them out, although now they go everywhere on tractors and their homes are in neat modern villas. One aspect of the landscape which he would find changed, although highly relevant, is represented by the scores of military cemeteries, each one individual in design and distinct from the rest, though each with those same rows of white headstones and the same Cross of Sacrifice, and each superbly tended by the gardeners of the Commonwealth War Graves Commission, forming unmistakable gardens of remembrance to the 250,000 British and Commonwealth soldiers who died in the Ypres Salient.

YPRES. — *La Grand'place un jour de marche.*

This page and opposite: *The three ages of twentieth-century man: The Grote Markt (Grand'Place) and the Cloth Hall in Ypres, just before the First World War, during its years of destruction and as it is today.*

CHAPTER 1

Peace Before the Plunge

Much has been written by historians and other authors, reflecting on how the conflict which began in August 1914 and which was to convulse much of the European continent for the next four years was a cataclysm separating the two very different worlds of before and after the war. My father, Alfred William Hall (Alf to most, including his wife-to-be, but often Bill, sometimes 'Nobby' and 'Curly' to a few), was one of those who lived through those times, so different from the world we know today. He was born on 2 February 1891 in south-east London and thus he spent his childhood and grew to manhood in that pre-war world which we today can only try to imagine and which was first undermined by the social changes born of the burgeoning technology of those days and then swept away by the eruptions of war. In the thirteen years which separated the death of Victoria from the more violent deaths of the Archduke and Archduchess of Austria-Hungary at Sarajevo, he evolved from a schoolboy into a young man who was beginning to find his feet in the commercial world of London, then the prosperous centre of a prosperous British Empire. His life, however, was ordained to be brusquely interrupted, as were those of millions of his generation of many lands around the globe, whose unique, unsought and unenviable destiny it was to be summoned to fight on the bloody battlefields of the bloodiest war mankind has ever seen.

Like so many, he volunteered in the very early weeks of the war – a war which was to see some 900,000 of his compatriots lose their lives and many more maimed for life. Therefore, when the end at last arrived four years later, he could count himself among the lucky survivors. They were, however, four years which had been stolen from the prime of his life, while for the greater part of that time he had been deprived of his liberty, at the mercy of his country's enemies. Only those on whom war has inflicted a similar indignity can appreciate what such an experience must mean to a young man who had not long embarked on adult life, with ideas and expectations, hopes and ambitions, and with the reasonable assumption that he would be allowed to pursue his course without interference from such an immense event as that which was coming to engulf him and his contemporaries.

He was a keen sportsman, which in those days of narrower opportunity largely meant football and cricket, while his formal education, as with most people in those times who were not born of rich parents, he could claim as being no more than basic, coming to an end at about the age of twelve. Nevertheless, having a taste for intellectual nourishment, he was at pains to continue it on a more informal basis for the rest of his life. Whether, by then, his reading had introduced him to the handsome and historic Belgian town of Ypres must be subject to doubt, but the time was coming when its name would assume a vast significance, for him and for the entire generation to which he belonged.

During the early years of the twentieth century, as my father emerged from childhood and moved towards the door into the adult world, the statesmen of Europe were, as usual, preoccupied with their wary manoeuvrings and disputes, not only concerning events on that continent, but also and not infrequently featuring colonies or – particularly in Germany's case – the relative lack of them. In 1905, she clashed with France over the latter's assumption of hegemony over the North African kingdom of Morocco. Along with other states, Great Britain was drawn into the argument. A conference found in favour of France, forcing Germany to back down, but the affair was a warning: Germany too wanted, as she put it, her 'place in the sun'.

In 1910, the 'Edwardian era' died, with the pleasure-loving king who gave it its name, and the more austere George V succeeded to the throne. The nineteen-year-old Alfred Hall had his own preoccupations; that summer he was turning out for the Glenville Cricket Club, ending the summer at the top of the bowling averages, for which he was awarded the 'First Bowling Prize'.

A year later, Morocco was the subject of further belligerent machinations by Germany, when its gunboat *Panther* appeared off the Moroccan port of Agadir, once more threatening French interests in that area. Telegrams flew back and forth between the nations and swords were again half-drawn from their scabbards. In the end, however, the argument was settled by diplomacy and a treaty was drawn up and signed. Nevertheless, in Europe the battle-lines were being drawn, with Germany and Austria-Hungary in one camp and Great Britain, France and Russia in the other. In particular, there was in this country a dawning perception that Germany was the threat to the peace which Europe had, in the main, so long enjoyed and a certain anti-German feeling began to take root in the people's minds. France, of course, with bitter memories of 1871, was in no doubt of the menace posed by the hated enemy, who ever since that time had been camped in force on the west bank of the Rhine, occupying the lost French provinces of Alsace and Lorraine. The possibility of some kind of European war began gradually to take shape.

Both France and Germany, through their long-established tradition of compulsory military service, could swiftly put large armies into the field, once mobilisation was declared. Great Britain, by contrast, kept only a small, professional army – the 'contemptible little army' in the German Kaiser's dismissive words – and, surrounded by the protecting sea, trusted in the Royal Navy for its security. But, to British dismay, the Prussian bully, that *parvenu* among nations and owner of the most powerful army in the world, was not only rattling his sabre, but also from 1908 beginning to engage in an ambitious warship-building programme, whose clear aim was to challenge the Royal Navy's long-established command of the world's oceans. An international competition was initiated, as Great Britain sought, with some reluctance, to maintain its superior position in the face of German naval aspirations.

For its part, the British Army, small though it was, had been subjected by the then Minister for War, Richard Burdon (later Lord) Haldane, to far-reaching reforms, based on his belief that its current structure, founded on the needs presented by the nation's nineteenth-century imperial wars against poorly-armed natives, was inappropriate for the modern warfare which it might have to face if called upon to fight a first-class European army. A part of his new policy – and of fundamental importance to it – had been the formation, in 1907, of a volunteer, part-time corps, called the Territorial Force, based on the traditions and, to some extent, on the membership of the old Yeomanry Companies. As 'Territorials', their express function was to garrison the island – and defend it if need be – while the regular army was campaigning overseas. There was no question, however, of copying the Continentals and introducing conscription; the Island was still an island – and it still had its Navy.

As it happened, when war eventually came, it was found that these arrangements could not be sustained and, before 1914 had reached its end, the first Territorial battalions were to be found manning the battle-lines across the Channel, in equal hazard with their 'regular' brothers-in-arms, as well as – and indeed well before – the men of Kitchener's 'New Armies'.

So we come to 1914 and the last days of the old peace. As July of that fateful year drew to a close, the statesmen had already been struggling for over a month with an international situation which, bringing terrible reality to Bismarck's prescient suggestion that a future European war might result from 'some damned silly thing in the Balkans', was gradually evolving into an apparently unstoppable slide into a general conflict. For the moment, ultimatums, rather than shot, were flying, but, as the statesmen strove for peace, whilst ever-mindful of their country's dignity, the sands were running out. In the end, diplomacy gave up the unequal struggle and, as one by one the dominoes fell, peace succumbed to irresistible forces and the lands of Europe slipped into war. Austria led the way against Serbia on 28 July, followed by

The 11th Battalion, County of London Regiment (the Finsbury Rifles), of the Territorial Force, at Okehampton in 1914.

Germany and Russia on 1 August. That same day, France mobilised her army and Britain sent her fleet to its wartime base at Scapa Flow.

On 3 August, with the guns already thundering in Serbia and Poland, France joined the combatants and marched her soldiers northwards and eastwards. The next day, as German troops poured into Belgium, Whitehall sent a final warning to the Wilhelmstrasse. When this failed to evoke a satisfactory answer, the last few hours of the old world were sent all too heedlessly to join the past. By midnight, the crowds thronging central London were cheering the news that Great Britain too had slipped its moorings and was moving out into the flood tide which, by the time it turned, would have swept away political and social settlements, ancient thrones and millions of lives.

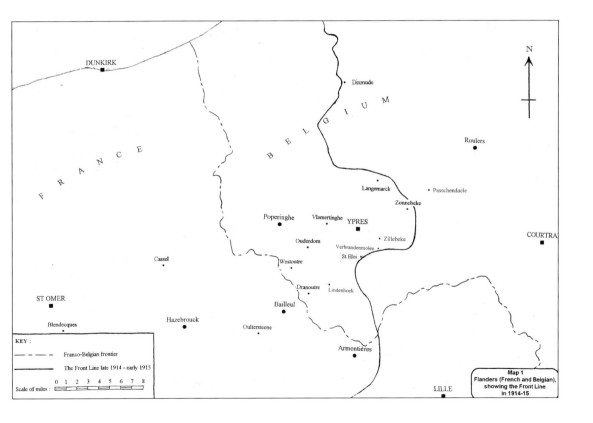

Map 1
Flanders (French and Belgian),
showing the Front Line
in 1914-15

CHAPTER 2
A Distant Drum

The British Expeditionary Force (BEF), under the command of Field Marshal Sir John French, crossed to France during August and moved up to assist in confronting the German right wing, already swinging through Belgium in accordance with the long-established Schlieffen Plan, which had as its object the encirclement and taking of Paris, as in 1870. Meanwhile, the French had lost no time in launching a full-scale attack in the east, in search of *la gloire* and the 'lost provinces', an enterprise which met with small success and heavy losses, while the Allies' left wing in Flanders and Champagne found itself having to fall back before massive German attacks, which were pressed home with an apparent indifference to casualties. Having scarcely arrived at the Belgian town of Mons, to an enthusiastic welcome from the local population, the BEF found itself almost at once obliged to retreat, though not without taking heavy toll of the grey-clad masses which advanced, in seemingly inexhaustible numbers, to confront the disciplined and accurate marksmanship of the British lines. As was to be the case a quarter of a century later, the Allies were rolled back in disorder towards Paris. By contrast with that latter occasion, however, the French determined to fight for their city and turned and opposed their would-be conquerors on the line of the River Marne. The Germans in their turn were forced to fall back, Paris was saved, the Channel ports were denied to the enemy and, with both sides temporarily exhausted from the ferocious fighting of those early months, they began the process of 'digging in' along a front which, from the Channel coast, ran southwards through the marshy lands of Flanders, crossing the River Somme and thence bending eastwards, in front of the French fortress of Verdun, until it ended at the Swiss border. The northern end of the line started at the sea near Nieuport and thence followed the defensive moat formed by the Yser Canal until it neared the medieval weaving town of Ypres. With most of Belgium overrun and only the south-western corner of that small nation, for whom we had notionally gone to war, remaining in Allied hands, the decision was taken, with the war but a few months old and little inkling of the years and trials which stretched ahead before peace would return, that Ypres should be defended from the German jackboot. Given the points to the north and south at which the Allied counter-attack had eventually been halted, this inevitably meant that there was a bulge in the line. Thus was born the 'immortal Salient', which was to be held against all the enemy's assaults until final victory four years later, although by then the town itself, surrounded on three sides by hostile artillery, had been reduced to little more than rubble. It was the defence of this area which became part of the responsibility of the BEF, along with units of the French army on its left flank, while the remainder of the line northwards to the coast was held by the small Belgian army.

LA MAISON DE VILLE

ESTAMINET

STATION DU TRAM

CAMPAGNE DE 1914 - POPERINGHE
Infanterie Anglaise sur la Grand'Place

Edit. Sansen-Vanneste, Poperinghe

Units of the BEF marching through Poperinghe in 1914.

By this time, much slaughter had taken place: the machine gun and the artillery piece had confirmed their status as mistresses of the field. Against their fearful power, friend and foe alike were obliged to seek shelter in the earth. The more familiar war of movement was replaced by a static one which seized the opposing armies in its hideous clamps. The trenches, that enduring symbol of the war of 1914–1918, were born, the euphoric optimism embodied in the expectant phrase 'home by Christmas' had died and the process began by which a substantial proportion of the young men of Europe were to find themselves funnelled into a semi-troglodytic and lethal hell, lasting for four whole years.

At Mons and Le Cateau in the previous August, although the professional soldiers of the BEF had fought magnificently, their bravery equalled by a superb standard of marksmanship and rate of fire, their losses had been grievous – losses made all the more significant by the fact that, compared with the huge conscripted armies of the other nations, their original numbers had been so small. As this country found itself engaged in full-scale war on the European continent for the first time in a hundred years and the awful nature of that war began to reveal itself, more and more manpower had to be demanded, to fill the gaps torn in the ranks by the high-explosive shell and the machine-gun bullet. With the war scarcely a month old and casualties already past the 10,000 mark, Field Marshal Lord Kitchener, now himself Minister for War, issued his celebrated (and now much-parodied) call to arms. The response reflected the widespread patriotic and anti-German mood of the nation: in those last five months of 1914, over one million volunteers joined the colours.

The clear-sighted Kitchener, already foreseeing the prospect of a long war, proposed the formation of a 'New Army' of citizen soldiers, which would swell and augment the existing Regular battalions and meet the needs of such a long conflict, although the Fates ordained that he himself would not live to see its end. In support of this aim, he also, as early as 7 August, wrote to the chairmen of the Territorial Force Associations around the country, requesting their help – not, as might be thought, in recruiting to the Territorial Force itself, but in encouraging existing members of Territorial battalions to transfer to the Regular Army. If that was evidence that he was less than enthusiastic about employing the Territorials as front-line units, his was a view not infrequently to be found amongst Regular soldiers. It is, however, a fact that, even on the day war was declared, the Territorial battalions were able to offer the nation over a quarter of a million men, trained at least in the military rudiments and mustered in their local battalions, with the valuable *esprit de corps* which the latter arrangement confers. At any rate, some 35,000 of the new volunteers preferred to enlist in their local Territorial unit, Alfred Hall being one of those who chose this way to serve their country. On 7 September, the day after the Allies began the counter-attack which has gone down in history as the Battle of the Marne and which was to drive the German army back from the gates of Paris, he enlisted in his own local formation, the 12th Battalion of the London Regiment, known as 'The Rangers', which had, like its many sister battalions, been in existence since the foundation of the Territorial Force. Although, as has already been noted,

Field Marshal the Earl Kitchener of Khartoum.

Men of the Rangers pose, bayonets fixed, date unknown.

The Rangers marching past the Polytechnic College, Regent Street, on Sunday, 2 August 1914, on their way to Waterloo station, bound for their annual training camp. (IWM Q71255)

While at Byfleet, Rifleman Hall had his photo taken, then, in buoyant mood, used it as a postcard to send to his mother.

19/11/14.

POST CARD

This space for communication | The address to be written here

Dr Ma.!
  Ow are yer?
We are still jogging
along here in the same
old way. Sometimes
cold sometimes hot.
but always happy.
Would very much like
to come up & see you
all. Leaving here shortly
for goodness knows
where Love to all
          aef

Mrs Hall
103 Murray St
New North Rd.
London
    N

Cpl C.W. Comber guarding the railway bridge at Byfleet, Surrey. On 14 February 1915, he was killed near Ypres – one of the Rangers' first casualties.

the Territorials were not intended to serve overseas, the crippling losses suffered and continuing to be suffered by the old professional army, as it encountered the new sort of warfare, were to render their presence in the fighting line in France imperative. Thus, at a very early stage of the war, with Kitchener's New Army of volunteers yet to achieve reality and while general conscription was still another two years away, the first of the Territorial battalions were called upon to take their places alongside their professional comrades. (The rules required that they should be asked to volunteer, but that did not seem to constitute an obstacle in the majority of cases.) First to reach France were the Oxfordshire Hussars and the London Scottish, in time to take part in the First Battle of Ypres, in October–November 1914.

The Rangers took a little longer to join the fighting: on 2 August – a Sunday – as the nation was grasping the truth that war was nearly upon them, they had paraded in Gray's Inn Square, watched by Bank Holiday crowds, preparatory to marching off to Waterloo, from where they planned to travel by rail to their annual training camp at Wool, in Dorset, as they had done in preceding summers. Their journey was nearly accomplished when orders came for them to turn round and return whence they came. Back in the capital they found themselves dismissed, to make an unexpected reappearance on the doorsteps of their respective homes, there to await a further summons, as those last momentous days passed into history.

Once mobilisation had been put in train, on 4 August, the 12th Londons spent some time at different training camps in and around the metropolis, moving out in September to Crowborough, Sussex. They now bore the official designation of the

AN APPEAL.

The Germans and their allies, with their millions of trained soldiers, have banded themselves together to annihilate our race. This they said themselves, and they go on saying it. They began the war by invading Belgium—a peaceful country inhabited by peaceful and industrious people— whose neutrality the Germans themselves had sworn to defend.

Belgium to-day is a waste land: her cities, universities, churches in ruins— her cottages and homesteads burnt to the ground. Thousands of men, women and children have been slaughtered; hundreds of thousands have fled from their country; those who still remain in Belgium are trodden under the heel of a foreign oppressor. They are either starving or in danger of starvation.

What will happen if the Germans invade Great Britain?

Atrocities even more terrible than those in Belgium will be perpetrated here. Women will see their fathers, their husbands, their brothers, their children shot down before their eyes; they themselves will be subject to the vilest infamy.

Men of Great Britain! are you waiting to see these sights in your own country?

Your fellow countrymen are giving their lives in the trenches to preserve your homes from invasion. They have been fighting against tremendous odds, shedding their blood freely in our defence. And when they call upon us for help shall we refuse to come to their aid?

Surely it is time for us to stand shoulder to shoulder in defence of our liberty, of our homes, of our very existence.

This leaflet represents a stark illustration of the current mood of the nation, both of the authorities who issued it and of the thousands who responded.

1/12 Londons, to differentiate them from a second battalion – the 2/12 – which had quickly been raised to form the new Home Battalion, this being based at the regimental headquarters in Chenies Street, just off Tottenham Court Road. By mid-October the 1/12 was quartered at Byfleet, Surrey, where the newly-enlisted Alfred Hall joined them. For the next two months, they found themselves engaged in their proper duties, guarding various sensitive points on the railway line between Waterloo and Aldershot. On 16 December, however, these duties came to an end: renewed fighting across the Channel, further long casualty lists and the French insistence that Britain should man a greater and more equitable share of the long battle line meant more fighting men were needed. Some of these – whatever Kitchener's reservations – had to be drawn from the Territorial Force and this time the Rangers were among the battalions selected to cross the water and join the BEF in France. At seven o'clock on the morning of 23 December, led by their newly appointed Commanding Officer, Lt-Col. A.D. Bayliffe, they entrained at Barnes station, en route for Southampton, where on the evening of the next day they embarked in the SS *Oxonian*, bound for France. After an overnight crossing on a calm, moonlit sea, the battalion disembarked at Le Havre on the morning of Christmas Day. Some Christmas!

From the docks, the Rangers marched off to No. 1 Rest Camp, on the outskirts of the town, where they were accommodated under canvas. For the next few days, while steady rain slowly turned the entire camp into a quagmire, the battalion found itself employed on fatigues in the dockyard – a dreary and dispiriting introduction to war. Fresh orders soon arrived and on the morning of the 29th all ranks paraded in the mud and the pouring rain – some of it turning to hail – preparatory to entraining for the BEF headquarters town of St Omer, some 30 miles west of the front line. There then ensued a wearisome journey by cattle truck, which was not ended until the morning of the next day when, having finally arrived, they marched to the village of Blendecques, on the outskirts of St Omer, where they were to be quartered for the next month. At that time, the battalion's strength stood at 30 officers and 856 other ranks, including Rifleman Hall in the ranks of 'C' Company.

Their time was spent in training, with much route-marching, practice in trench-digging under the supervision of an RE major and practice firing on the local range. On 27 January, they were moved further east to Hazebrouck, to be embodied in the 27th Division. On arrival, however, they found no billets prepared, as the Divisional Staff seemed unaware of their existence. The Battalion War Diary, written up every day by Col. Bayliffe mostly in pencil on 'Army form C.2118' reports thus:

> 2.30 pm   Battalion arrived. OC Billeting party reported he had arrived 12 midday and was told battalion not expected and no billeting arranged for or obtainable and that Town Commandant was absent for day.
>
> 3.0 pm   I reported to HQ Second Army. Was informed they had no instructions with regard to battalion. Saw Staff Captain V Corps who took me to partially built hospital where I decided to billet. He told me to report at HQ V Corps.
>
> 5.0 pm   Reported HQ V Corps. Saw GOC who told me we were to go to 28th Division who had been warned to send me orders for tomorrow's move.

The next day, on a frosty January morning, the unwanted 1/12 paraded outside what had been an unduly dirty and uncomfortable night's lodging. From there, they were quickly moved on, marching along icy roads to the village of Oultersteene, where they found themselves part of 85 Brigade of the 28th Division and quartered in much improved billets in farm buildings. On 2 February, as the battalion

[*This paper is to be considered by each soldier as confidential, and to be kept in his Active Service Pay Book.*]

You are ordered abroad as a soldier of the King to help our French comrades against the invasion of a common Enemy. You have to perform a task which will need your courage, your energy, your patience. Remember that the honour of the British Army depends on your individual conduct. It will be your duty not only to set an example of discipline and perfect steadiness under fire but also to maintain the most friendly relations with those whom you are helping in this struggle. The operations in which you are engaged will, for the most part, take place in a friendly country, and you can do your own country no better service than in showing yourself in France and Belgium in the true character of a British soldier.

Be invariably courteous, considerate and kind. Never do anything likely to injure or destroy property,

H W V

2

and always look upon looting as a disgraceful act. You are sure to meet with a welcome and to be trusted; your conduct must justify that welcome and that trust. Your duty cannot be done unless your health is sound. So keep constantly on your guard against any excesses. In this new experience you may find temptations both in wine and women. You must entirely resist both temptations, and, while treating all women with perfect courtesy, you should avoid any intimacy.

Do your duty bravely.
Fear God.
Honour the King.

KITCHENER,
Field-Marshal.

Lord Kitchener's own moral philosophies are much to the fore in this exhortation which was issued to every soldier posted overseas.

proceeded at the rear of the Divisional train to Ouderdom, Rifleman Hall celebrated his twenty-fourth birthday in the course of an uncomfortable march, which was probably alleviated, as was usual in those days, by choral renderings of popular favourites such as 'Tipperary', 'Pack up your Troubles' and possibly a vocal reference to a certain Mademoiselle from the town of Armentières, which lay in the war zone on the Allied side of the lines, a few miles away to the south-east. At Ouderdom, billeting arrangements seemed once more to have gone awry. Darkness had fallen by the time temporary homes in farm buildings were at last found for the weary troops. Their progress had gradually taken them ever nearer the sound of the guns and the realities of war. They had that day in fact crossed into Belgium, or that small part of it which remained under Allied control. A few days later, they were to find themselves in Ypres itself. As, in the new world in which he found himself, my father began to discover in himself a quickening interest in foreign languages, he will have been amongst those who had noticed that some of the village names, hitherto of a French aspect, now seemed to be composed of the rather stranger combinations of letters – to an English eye – which mark the Flemish language.

CHAPTER 3

In the Salient

The countryside which formed the Ypres Salient is of an open and gently undulating nature, being divided by a series of low 'ridges' running roughly east-west, alternating with small streams, called 'beeks', which flow from east to west. This whole area is enclosed on the north and east by a somewhat higher ridge, which, running in a north-south line, forms a northerly continuation of the Messines ridge, before curving round to the north-west. As ridges go, it is of no great altitude – at its highest points it is never as much as 200 feet above sea level – but possession of even such a modest elevation placed its owner in a position of advantage, particularly in the case of the German forces, whose resources in artillery – and the shells for it to fire – were greatly superior to those of the British. The transverse ridges are even lower (for example, from the top of the Gravenstafel ridge to the bed of the Haanebeek near St Julien, the drop scarcely amounts to 50 feet). Nevertheless, contention for their possession was to result in much fighting, with heavy losses on both sides.

As for the effects of war, in that first quarter of 1915 the area was yet to be reduced by continuous warfare to that bare and desolate landscape which has become the most abiding image of the First World War battlefields. Pastures were still grassed, trees and hedges yet survived and, even though shells whistled regularly over their heads, some farmers were still doggedly working their fields and clinging to their homes, either isolated or in the small villages, such as St Jean, Velorenhoek or Wieltje, which dotted the land.

Although the countryside had so far been spared – at least by comparison with what it was to suffer later – Ypres itself had not. The first shells had landed in the town's main square, the Grande Place, on 7 October 1914 and the town had continued to suffer the attentions of the enemy's artillery ever since. The magnificent Cloth Hall, dating from the thirteenth century, still stood, but, along with the town's other fine buildings, had received a number of direct hits and was already well on the way to that state of almost total destruction in which it ended the war.

The Rangers had now been in the war zone for some six weeks, long enough to become accustomed to their new lives. During that time, more units, both Regular and TF, had been continually arriving, as the British sought to put ever more men in the field, to shoulder what their French ally felt would be a fairer proportion of the burden. Among them was the 1st Battalion of the Suffolk Regiment, whose ranks were destined to be closely associated with the men of the Rangers, both on the field of battle and in the prison camp. Summoned back from pre-war duties in the Sudan, they had landed at Le Havre on 18 January. Being Regulars, they were regarded as needing less preparation for combat than their Territorial comrades, so it was only three weeks later, on 4 February, while the Rangers were still training in the back areas, that they found themselves manning front-line trenches near the southern edge of the Salient. One of their number, Pte H.J. Clarke, a signaller, who later on, after he had been taken prisoner, wrote up an account of his experiences in a small notebook, describes therein that first excursion to the firing zone, not far from where the Rangers, too, were soon to be sent:

> ...*started out for our first tour in the trenches, rather a long and dismal march, between 3 and 3½ kilometres, made a halt at Blauwepoort Farm and there began our casualties, distance from the trenches about 1500 yards, Ptes Palfrey and Cook being wounded, stray shots falling all over the place, no more casualties before reaching trenches, relieved Cheshire Regt about 1 am the 5th, everything being settled by daybreak. Hdqrs at Verbrandenmolen, 600 yards in rear of firing line, that being my first position, nothing much occurred until towards dusk, rifle fire gradually creeping up into a regular hurricane causing no amount of wind and also our first casualties in the trenches, Pte Horace Nunn, grenade thrower, being our first man killed, then followed Pte Philips, one of my own particular chums, Number 7437. Our first 48 hours in were not what could be termed bad, we were then relieved by Cheshires during night and early morn of 6th/7th, falling back again into supports with 'A' and 'C' Coys at Blauwepoort Farm with 'B', 'D' and Hdqrs at Infantry Bks.*

A few days later, after the briefest of rests, the Suffolks were ordered back to the line, as Clarke reports, in his own informal and animated style:

> *Awful time altogether, a position to the right of the line with Yser Canal running through centre and just through Zillebeke. Trenches had to be reached by crossing open ground, heavy firing preventing us from getting near trenches until 2 am 17th. We were more or less prepared for a good reception, due to men belonging to East Surreys now and then intermixed with a few Middlesex passing us on our way up, all in an awful state and shouting we are all that is left of our respective Regts, also what a '*Hell*' it was, one party even asked for our names and addresses so as to be able to let our people know that we were gone under, had indeed had a rough time so could easily be excused (at least by those who have seen for themselves as we eventually did). Our reception was indeed good on nearing our goal, machine guns etc creating a terrible din. Our Regiment suffered heavily that night and morning, being attached to Hdqrs again was indeed fortunate for me, my Company through some unforeseen thing happening were taken straight to enemy's lines after leaving Hdqrs, only 43 being accounted out of 198. Should have occupied 'O' trench but on arrival met with a hot reception from Gs, Hand-grenades, Jam-tins, etc, being received by them when within 12 yards range, Captain Jourdain in command being killed, Captain Campbell with Lt Payne returning somehow or other wounded, Ptes Bloomfield (7502) also Ansell (7540) also returning wounded, all to their rear. Lieut Moysey with Lieut Biggs being taken prisoners with about 100 to 120 men (have since met Ptes Waspe and Haylock who were amongst them at Giessen Camp but not being in my Company could not have much to say to them). Northumberland Fusiliers came up to relieve us on night of 17th, Corpl Crabb, myself and 4 others being detailed to lay communication wire for them, again lucky for us to be in rear*

for on gaining open ground came in for another drink from their Machine Guns, wiping the first two platoons out completely. Threw ourselves down and waited till things had quieted down again, started off again across turnip field or what was then a field of dead, bodies being strewn all over the place. By this time we had gradually worked our way up to the front so as to have communication established, Gs then successfully lighted barns to our rear and our left, thereby showing everything around as clear as daylight. Down we went again, being completely buried in mud whilst our <u>friends</u> on the other side sent over a fusillade of bullets with occasional shells, there we laid for roughly $1\frac{1}{2}$ hours, so after communicating with our Hdqrs and finding it impossible to advance the order was given to retire, led back by Officer of East Surreys who received Silver Cross for good work done that night.

As for the Rangers, their first view of Ypres came on the evening of 8 February, when they marched for the first time along its rubble-strewn streets, seeing for themselves the state of the abused and beleaguered town. Darkness had fallen by the time that, along with numbers of others, they found themselves quartered within the massive walls of the Cavalry Barracks. After a couple of days occupied with 'fatigues', the battalion began to experience its first taste of the front line, though not yet in a combatant role. As raw newcomers, they were allotted tasks of a supporting nature – in particular the finding of parties for carrying rations and ammunition up to the men in the trenches. With communications trenches largely absent in those early days, this was necessarily done in the open and hence necessarily at night – by no means easy work – in the dark, for long hours, over broken and unfamiliar country, very muddy in places and with the front line at that time still several miles from the city gates. As well as arduous, the work could also be dangerous for, although night afforded a cloak to their activities, their journeyings were exposed to the random nocturnal firing which the enemy was always liable to let off from his points of vantage.

It was not long after their arrival in Ypres that the Rangers recorded their first official encounter with the Suffolks, though it was to be in the least happy of circumstances. One night, a Rangers man taking his turn as sentry at the Barracks in Ypres discerned a figure approaching through the gloom. The sentry, no doubt nervous and certainly inexperienced, issued the appropriate challenge. When no answer came, he did his duty, fired at the unknown and a certain Pte Ward fell fatally wounded, to join the Suffolks' swelling casualty list.

A few more days went by and then at last, on the night of 12/13 February, the 12th Londons found themselves in the war proper, with A and C Companies ordered to take their places in the trenches for 24 hours, being relieved by B and D Companies the following night.

At that point in the war, the trenches had not become the more sophisticated earthworks of later on, nor in that sector of the line could they be very deep. At the eastern tip of the Salient, the line ran along the main ridge, where conditions were somewhat drier, but elsewhere it descended to the lower ground where the water table was nearer the surface and any digging which went further down than about four feet soon became waterlogged. To get the full height necessary for safety, the parapet had to be built up with sand-bags, while more often than not the bottom of the trench became a quagmire anyway. A number of men reported sick with either frost bite or trench foot while, for the Rangers, the pace began to quicken. On the 14th, the first casualties were suffered, with 2 men killed and 2 others wounded. Early on the 15th the War Diary reported:

> 5 am   *By order of GOC 85 Bde, 2 Platoons No 1 Coy were ordered to proceed to CHATEAU LANKOF, there to collect rations water and ammunition and carry them to No 2 Coy in trench S. Remainder No 1 Coy (less 2 Platoons) ordered to proceed to St ELOI and establish communication between left of 27 Div. and right of 28 Div.*

These activities resulted in further casualties, with 3 officers and 7 other ranks killed, while the rain continued to fall and the mud continued to prosper. On the 16th the battalion was moved to the rear area for a period of rest, first to Ouderdom and then to Hoeksken, between Vlamertinghe and Poperinghe. This, however, was not accomplished without some further military confusion. Col. Bayliffe recorded it thus in the War Diary:

> 11.30 am *Informed by MMP at crossroads here that road leading N into my billeting area was closed to transport which would have to move via WESTOUTRE and BOESCHEPE entailing a march of $6\frac{1}{2}$ miles in lieu of 3.*
> *No march route was given me, nor was I warned that any roads were closed to transport.*
> 1.30 pm *Battalion arrived DERYCKES FARM, Poperinghe.*

Confusion continued: within 24 hours orders came that the battalion was to return to Ypres:

> 1.0 pm   *At No 22 Rue Lombard, YPRES.*
> *Saw Town Commandant and arranged for billeting of battalion near Railway Station.*
> *Fighting strength: 20 Off., 698 ORs.*

A and D Companies went straight to the trenches, with the other two in reserve. For once, a sunny day gave promise of some relief from the wet and the cold.

Another 24 hours passed, then the army changed its mind again; once more the Rangers returned to Poperinghe, this time for a real rest, lasting for over a week. At that time Poperinghe had not long been taken over from the French, as part of the extension of the front for which the British Army was assuming responsibility. Lying less than 10 miles west of Ypres, Poperinghe was reached in those days by a tree-lined, frequently shelled road which ran eastwards through the village of Vlamertinghe and which all who served in the Salient trod at some time or other, throughout the four years. In due time it was to become the centre of the main rest area for all the troops engaged in the Salient, as more rest camps like Deryckes Farm gradually mushroomed

The Rue de Lille, Ypres, after the fighting of 1915. Compare this with the pre-war photograph on page 2.

in the surrounding countryside, to receive tired bodies of men marching thankfully westwards away from Ypres for an all-too-short period of rest out of the line. In those early days of 1915, however, it was yet to achieve its later fame as the place, with its many cafés, restaurants and other solaces, where weary warriors, temporarily reprieved from the rigours of the trenches, could rediscover some of the lost pleasures of normal life – although, even there, the occasional enemy shell or bomb was prone to arrive, as a reminder of the war to which they must soon return. As for the famous Talbot House, or Toc H Club, run by the army padre 'Tubby' Clayton, that sanctuary was not destined to open its doors for another nine months.

On 1 March, at the rather late hour of 6.30 p.m., orders were received that C Company was to report to OC 1/Royal Scots Fusiliers that same night. The rest of the battalion was similarly sent into the trenches alongside other Regular battalions, an arrangement which was designed to further their practical education in the arts of war, 1915 style, under the expert tutelage of the soldiers they had been sent to join. As they made their way forward, lowering skies and falling temperatures seemed to threaten snow, a promise which was fulfilled with the arrival of a heavy fall on the following afternoon, to add to the miserable conditions afforded by the mud and water already covering the floor of the trenches. A few days later, their period of training over and united once more, they marched thankfully back for a further period of rest in their old home at Deryckes Farm. There, early on the morning of 10 March, they heard the thunder of guns to the south, telling of the opening of the three-day battle of Neuve Chapelle, a costly episode they were able to evade. Fate was reserving them for the next, longer and even bloodier battle, in the Salient itself.

Further casualties had meanwhile been suffered, with 4 more officers and 16 other ranks killed and 2 officers and 34 other ranks wounded. These, together with other losses due to sickness, were made good during February and March by several drafts of replacements which came out from the 2nd Battalion at home.

During these days the Rangers found themselves frequently shuffled from place to place: Vlamertinghe, Bailleul and Dranoutre all knew their presence, with working parties being sent up from the last-named village to the trenches in front of Lindenhoek. The arrival of Easter in early April found some of them in those trenches, but the battalion was never left in one place for long and on Easter Saturday it was moved once more, to Ravelsburg, once more in reserve. There, on the following Tuesday, the opportunity was taken to hold a Battalion Sports Day, a valuable relief from the rigours and discomfort of the previous three months' events. It would not, however, have been the Army if such pleasurable occasions had been allowed to pass without the imposition of inspection parades – the first one on the following day by the GOC 2nd Army, General Sir Horace Smith-Dorrien, after which the battalion marched in the pouring rain to fresh billets in Bailleul. Here, a second inspection was imposed, this time by Smith-Dorrien's subordinate – and not to be outdone – their own V Corps commander, Lt-Gen. Sir Herbert Plumer.

A few days later, they moved once more to Vlamertinghe where, finding themselves billeted near to their peacetime Territorial comrades, the 9th London Regiment (Queen Victoria's Rifles), time was found for a football match between the two battalions (Rangers 2, Queen Victoria's 0).

A scene in the village of Westoutre, before war arrived in its midst.

Dranoutre and Bailleul, two more places on the 1/12th's peregrinations.

The countryside in the Salient, as it looked in July 1915. This view was taken from Wieltje, facing NNW towards St Julien. (IWM Q37695)

The Rue du Marché au Beurre in Ypres, also in 1915.

Dead horses lying outside the Cathedral of St Martin, Ypres, in March 1915. (IWM Q61643)

Damaged farmhouse in the Salient, in March 1915. (IWM Q61606)

This trench, photographed in the Salient in March 1915, seems to be disused. Although apparently dry, it has typically been built up with sandbags, probably because the high water table would not allow the deeper excavation otherwise necessary. It also illustrates the relative unsophistication of those early days, before trench-digging had become something of an art. (IWM Q61595)

By 17 April, players and supporters alike had taken their separate ways back to the war, the 'Vics' to assist in the storming of Hill 60, while the Rangers returned north-wards and out to the tip of the Salient to take up positions in the firing line up on the main ridge at Broodseinde, just beyond the village of Zonnebeke, where they found the 1st Suffolks already installed on their immediate right:

> *Battn. moved to ZONNEBEKE – D Coy relieved Cheshires in trenches 17 & 18. C Coy relieved N Fusiliers in Trench 19. A Coy occupied Railway Dugouts. B Coy occupied Brick kilns.*

By now, the worst of the winter was over and some bright sunny days heralded the arrival of milder weather, though the nights were still very cold, particularly for those manning the trenches. By now, too, the men of the Rangers had seen something of war. If, on that far-off day at Christmastide, they had filed on to the decks of the *Oxonian* believing that they were bound simply for some new and exciting adventure, echoing the careless high spirits with which many young men went to the war in those early days, a more sober reality must now have seized their minds. For the first time in their lives, they had been confronted with the effects which modern high-explosive could have, both on flesh and on stone. Some of their companions with whom they had crossed the sea were now lying forever in the Flanders soil; tomorrow offered nothing but a new uncertainty.

These things they knew; other matters, of greater moment, lay beyond their ken. They were unaware, though would not have been surprised, that on both sides of the front line plans were being laid for new offensives. For his part, General Sir Douglas Haig, commanding the First Army from his GHQ in the 'White Chateau' on the Menin Road outside Ypres, was preparing a new attack south of the Salient, to be coordinated with action by the French, on his southern flank. However, the German generals also had plans for offensive operations, which included an attack on the Ypres Salient, defended by the British Second Army, of which V Corps – and the 12th London Regiment – were a part.

The enemy struck first, using a new and frightening weapon which technology was now offering. 22 April was a beautiful spring day, the Salient was going through one of its quieter periods and, although Ypres received more destructive high-explosive from the enemy artillery, in the fields to the east farmers were still stubbornly working. Thus matters stayed through the better part of the day, until a change in the weather conditions gave the enemy the chance for which he had been waiting. At about five o'clock, while the British Army, war or no war, was having its tea, a light wind began to blow from the north. At the same time, the German guns, which had been silent for a while, renewed their attentions, not only on the city but also on the countryside in the north-east sector of the Salient. Shortly thereafter, the crew of an aircraft of 6 Squadron Royal Flying Corps, on patrol over that part of the front, saw a yellowish cloud emerge from the German lines near Langemarck and, carried by the wind, slowly roll towards the opposing trenches, then held by two second-line French Divisions. On the right, next to the Canadians, were the 45th Algerians, newly-arrived in the line, and on their left flank, the 87th Territorials – composed of reservists – men no longer in their first youth, who had completed their full-time military service and whom the present emergency had pressed back into the ranks.

Although, some weeks previously, the Allies had received warnings of German intentions regarding the use of gas, these had been dismissed and no kind of protective equipment had been made available. Indeed, none was yet to hand, although some work had been done back in Britain to contrive and produce such devices. Thus, the hapless defenders, with no answer to the chlorine which choked their lungs, abandoned their line and fell back in disarray. Some, in their terror and physical discomfort, retreated so far that British troops in rest camps off the Ypres-Poperinghe road were astonished suddenly to see strange apparitions staggering towards them, gasping for air and in evident distress. Within a very short time, the flow of fugitives had become a flood, augmented by the remaining civilian inhabitants of the affected area, while a 4-mile gap had been torn in the defence line and the road to Ypres lay wide open. That the Salient was not overcome there and then was due partly to inadequate follow-up action by the attackers and partly to the heroism of such British troops as could be found, which were thrust hastily into the breach, to replace the shocked and demoralised French. As it was, at the end of a desperate, chaotic day, much ground had been lost and the Salient's northern defence line consisted of nothing more than isolated units, manned by tired

By the end of Second Ypres, the city had suffered grievously, yet, wrecked as it was by that time, its assailants contrived to achieve even more destruction before the conflict ended.

men in sadly depleted numbers, crouching in any shallow holes they had been able to scrape in the still-muddy ground or holding out in the ruins of cottages and farmhouses. Throughout the next day, what reserves that could be found were rushed up to fill the gaps, but the collapsed shape of the line thus formed was hardly one which tacticians would recommend, with, in particular, elements of the Canadian Division on the right in serious danger of being taken in the flank.

Hardly had steps been taken to guard against this when, two days later, the Germans used gas a second time. This time it was the men of the Canadian Division who bore the brunt. Although respirators had now been hastily ordered, none had yet arrived, so that the defenders were reduced to using whatever makeshift protection they could devise, usually a rag of some kind, wetted with any liquid which came to hand. Inevitably many were seriously affected and some retreated to the rear, but the majority in the two Canadian battalions most involved stuck to their posts and succeeded in holding off the German attack which followed the gas cloud, as it rolled southwards and gradually dispersed. Nevertheless, this second use of a new weapon, officially outlawed by the rules of warfare, inevitably accentuated the desperate nature of the situation. Once more a gap was opened in the British front line, to add to the perilous circumstances still pertaining on the left flank.

The Rangers were not immediately affected by these events. On the 22nd, they were still manning their trenches at Broodseinde to the south; then at 1 a.m. on the

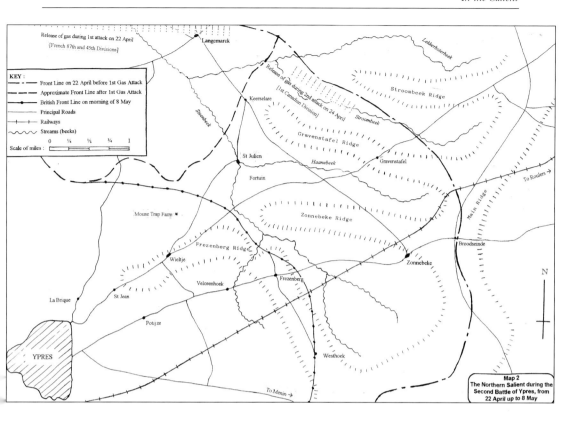

Map 2
The Northern Salient during the
Second Battle of Ypres, from
22 April up to 8 May

24th, some hours prior to the second gas attack, their week-long sojourn in the front line was ended by the arrival of their relief, in the shape of their fellow-Territorials, the 1st Monmouthshires, and the Londoners fell back to rest billets in Verlorenhoek. However, the desperate nature of the situation ordained that their rest was to be of the very shortest. Hardly had they arrived when a message came from Brigade, ordering them to be ready to move at a moment's notice, pending the receipt of further instructions to go forward once more, this time in company with the 1st Suffolks, the combined force to come under the orders of Col. Wallace commanding the latter battalion.

While awaiting his new orders, Col. Bayliffe decided that it would be worthwhile to send a young officer, Lt Hunter, accompanied by a signaller, to see if he could acquire some positive information which might help to dispel the mists shrouding the area into which it seemed he was going to have to advance. By the time Lt Hunter's written report reached Col. Bayliffe, by then wounded and out of the fight, the rush of events would have rendered it redundant, but it serves quite usefully to give a picture of the stage on to which the Rangers were about to step:

> *When I left you on Saturday morning [the 24th] I cycled to Wieltje and found that the village and roads entering it were being heavily shelled. I met and questioned several Canadians and others coming in from the firing line – they gave a very pessimistic account*

A German aerial photograph of gas being released.

of conditions there, which I thought was probably exaggerated. In one of the houses in the village I found Col Geddes who had charge of three Battalions and a certain sector of the line (I understood) and I thought he would be in touch with things. He gave me a situation report which I sent back to you by Cpl Piper. Shelling was increasing in intensity and presently the telephone line failed and no information was obtainable from the trenches. Col Geddes said that if I liked to go out and try to get into touch with some of the units in the firing line it would be of great use in clearing up the situation, as one of his battalions reported that they could not find anyone on their left. I went out to do what I could, but found that the job was a very difficult one, as the whole line was entirely open to the enemy's view, all buildings were being shelled and many were burning, hedges were systematically searched with shrapnel and on the slightest sign of movement on the St Jean – Wieltje Road, high explosive and shrapnel were turned on in apalling [sic] quantities. The fields leading up to this part of the line appeared all exposed to machine gun fire and quite impossible by daylight. I spotted a slight ridge to the left and decided to make for that along the road – keeping in the ditch as far as possible. Managed to get close up to this and found Royal Scots (T.F.) entrenched with their C.O. and H.Q. Staff in dug-outs close behind. The enemy's line could be seen in front of them and there was a gap of about 300 yards in our line between Royal Scots' right and a farm which they knew to be occupied by Canadians (evidently a small force who had taken up a position on the left of Col Geddes' people (The Buffs). Royal Scots were waiting until night to connect up with these. I crept along further to the left and found Col Tewson of D.C.L.I. in dug-out, behind the ridge with his trench line on left of Royal Scots and somewhat in advance of them. It was impossible to learn any more, so I returned to Wieltje to report to Col Geddes and to gather anything further that he had learnt.

There were no indications of further retirement so that I did not think it advisable to return to you until I had further information (in accordance with your instructions). During the time I was talking to Col Tewson I noticed an aeroplane of French shape, with the usual rings painted on wings, hovering over our neighbourhood. About 200 yards away were two of our field guns behind a hedge and well hidden. The 'plane passed over them, turned at right angles and dipped, then sailed off. A few minutes later half a dozen shells dropped around the guns (gunners fled to cover) and there was a direct hit on one of the limbers. There is very little doubt that this was a German machine – either a captured French one or a copy.

I think the Bosches must have seen somebody enter the house where Col Geddes was, for when I got back they had burnt a barn at the end of the garden and were busy crumping the houses on either side with a heavy howitzer and presently started on the one we were in. After about 20 minutes we were shelled out and had to bolt along to St. Jean. My bicycle and my orderly's were broken by shrapnel and had to be abandoned (they were outside the house in Wieltje). All along the road to St. Jean – although in small parties – we were followed with shrapnel. Here they had caught a wagon of an ammunition column and wiped the horses and drivers clean off the road with high explosive. From St. Jean I left Col Geddes and cut across country to Velorenhoek for orders. Found Battalion gone; reported to 85th Brigade, told them all I could; learnt approximate direction of advance, followed up (some hours behind). Got mixed up with some Canadian remnants, met some of our wounded coming back. We were badly shelled all the way and at the Fortuin Road they turned a machine gun on us and there

La Guerre Européenne 1914 — Turcos rejoignant pour faire la poursuite aux armées Prussiennes en retraite

Algerian troops – dubbed 'Turcos'.

Belgian Refugees fleeing before Germans   Réfugiés belges fuyant devant les Allemands

A scene repeated many times in the early months of the war, as the inhabitants vacated their native lands, henceforth to be claimed by the opposing armies for their exclusive use and its systematic destruction.

were many casualties. Young Brockis (who stuck to me all day) and I escaped and proceeded but could not locate the Battalion. Found an orderly of ours with an urgent message for Col Wallace of the Suffolks whom he could not find. I took him there – about a mile away. Col Wallace asked me personally to deliver his reply to his Adjutant. I therefore went back again to find Capt. Balders. During the day I had several heavy bursts very close by and was feeling very sick and my legs and ankles went groggy so that by the time I found the Suffolks I was about done up.

I discovered that our own people were digging in with the Suffolks a little way behind the firing line, to hold Fortuin. On my way there I met Hoare being helped back, wounded in the leg, but I don't think it was very serious. Afterwards Major Challen told me I could go back to Velorenhoek with Worthington to rest; when I reached there I am afraid I collapsed and that is all I remember until next day when I was rather a wreck.

While Lt Hunter was out on his reconnaissance, the orders for the Suffolks and the Rangers arrived. The latters' War Diary describes the subsequent events:

2pm *Order came from 85th Bde that Suffolks and ourselves were under their orders and were to advance towards FORTUIN 'and attack anything we met'. The message stated that FORTUIN was occupied by a mixed force of Germans of all arms and that OC Suffolks would command. OC Suffolks*

> came to my HQ and arranged order of attack and formation to be adopted,
> viz:- 4 lines of 1/2 battalions in extended order. He ordered me to move
> with my own battalion in support of the Suffolks.
>
> 2pm   *Battalion moved in extended order about 1000yds in N direction, then
> swung NE keeping FORTUIN on L. Front, turning NW again. Colonel
> hit during this time, Dug in facing ST JULIEN about 800 yds from it.
> Line straightened facing N and dug in again. Meanwhile 2 platoons of D
> Co and 1 platoon of Suffolks + Machine Gun under Capt Jones went into
> Canadian support trench N end of which was held by Germans and after
> dark (12.30) fell back rejoining line which reformed as follows:*
>
> *Rangers facing due N, Suffolks on L, Canadians on R facing NW. Sgt
> Garwood + 10 men with latter just N of Rd running from
> ZONNEBEKE W.N.W. Spent night making trenches on lines shown on
> map II which had originally been dugouts.*

Of necessity, a battalion war diary, composed under comfortless conditions, with other more immediate and urgent troubles besetting its author, himself not long released from the clamour and horror of battle, results in a most limited and imperfect impression of events. Nor can it, from the limited perspective of a battalion head-quarters, tell of the overall direction being taken by the fighting across the whole battlefield. Thus with the above entry; the gap rent in the northern line of the Salient by the gas attack had rendered the defenders on either side very vulnerable to flank attacks from the enemy exploiting it. Indeed, more than one position had been overrun and all in it killed or captured.

The situation was certainly confused. During the First World War, technology, in its faltering and imperfect state of progress, often set commanders worse problems than it solved. Communications were a major example: with radio still in its infancy and unavailable for general use, the only links between a general headquarters and units in the field, perhaps two or three miles away, were by telephone land-line or runner. All too frequently, the former tended to be destroyed by shellfire (in his report, Lt Hunter refers to a telephone line having failed) and signallers were continually to be found laying out new lines, often under conditions which were frequently both uncomfortable and hazardous. An entry in Clarke's diary referring to an earlier period graphically describes the laying of such telephone lines and the attendant difficulties:

Officer then explained we had got to lay wire to 'S' trench then occupied by Welsh Regt, none of us knowing the exact route turned it into rather a chance game on account of trenches not being all connected up, so proceeded by compass, proceeded about 100 yards over top of wood to the right then taking a direct turn to our left. Found an old commu-nication trench not far ahead so thought it best to get well under as we were now completely in the open. Tusky first ventured and finding himself submerged to the waist in mud and water did not stay long, we then followed this trench for about 250 yards when we were halted rather abruptly by someone shouting out (Get down you — Fools) and we were down wire and all before he had hardly finished his decent and expressive sentence. Then we were greeted with you are — lucky, but at least we had found our destination A.1. Officer in answer to his stating we were lucky answered we were rather cunning. Soon fixed up and off on our way back (my first view of the trenches) and I might say we stuck to the communication although up to our waists. Getting out of that we started on what I thought a decent game, testing every wire broken or otherwise that we could find. By the time we reached Hdqrs we had been at it for over 5 hours, thought we had finished but no such luck, for although there were others on our game at Hdqrs he wanted us to carry on with him to 'N' trench. Kicked off again but had only gone about 300 to 350 yards when OFR exclaimed (I am hit), had gone through his left calf, left telephone etc as he had to be carried back as stretchers were always in use, but managed him alright, finding my overcoat pocket filled with blood when putting him down. Felt extremely sorry for him as he seemed an awfully good fellow, but rather pleased at the prospect of finishing for the night for it turned out as such.

With the telephone lines often out of action, it was the runners who remained the only means of communication available – though a far slower one (and also not necessarily reliable, many being killed or injured on the way). No wonder the generals, encumbered by information concerning the situation which was often either incomplete or out-of-date – or indeed both – did not always seem to know what they were doing!

In the present situation, with the defences broken up by the gas attacks and reduced in some places to isolated groups, out of touch with their commanders and hanging on as best they could, the immediate and urgent need was for more fighting formations, to be thrown into the places where the gaps appeared to be – insofar as the location of such gaps could be determined. The Canadian Division, which had been bearing the brunt, had nothing left which was readily available, so Maj.-Gen. T.D'O. Snow (as the officer responsible on the spot) decided that *in extremis* he must take whatever lay to hand. Hence the order to the Suffolks and the Rangers to advance, although they were part of 28th Division, immediately to the south of the stricken sector. The urgency and the communications difficulties also decreed that it had to be done without reference to their Divisional Commander, Maj.-Gen. E.S. Bulfin.

It was under these conditions that the two battalions, under combined command and in a situation which was both desperate and confused, set off from Verlorenhoek in a north-easterly direction towards Fortuin, in response to orders which, thanks to the lack of a precise definition of the situation, were able to give them only the most generalised of instructions – 'attack anything we met'. Theirs not to reason why ...! The danger point was assumed to be the known gap in the line to the east of St Julien, where the area described as Fortuin lay, Col. Wallace having been informed that St Julien itself was still in our hands. In fact, the Germans had by then almost completely ejected its defenders and, from its now-ruined houses, commanded the open country on its eastern side. It was across this open farmland, lacking cover of any kind, that the Suffolks and Rangers were moving, up to and across the Wieltje-Gravenstafel road, meeting fire from all arms. As they advanced, they were met by an officer of the Canadian 2nd Brigade, under whose guidance they attempted to close up with the left of the Canadian 8th Battalion, the Winnipeg Rifles. They were now exposed, not only to enfilading machine gun fire from the enemy occupying St Julien, but to artillery fire as well. Some of the latter was coming from batteries on their own side which were unaware of their presence in the area – communications again – while more damage was created by the ever-present German artillery, and casualties in the two battalions mounted into three figures. By six o'clock the survivors were digging in due east of St Julien, near the small stream known as the Haanebeek, and clinging on grimly. Several other battalions, acting independently, had meanwhile come up on their left and, for the time being, further progress of the German onslaught was halted. After dark, the Suffolks and the Rangers were pulled back to the Wieltje-Gravenstafel road where, with the air still heavy with the smell of the gas released that morning, they dug in once more. There they stayed for 48 hours, lonely and exposed, enduring further casualties from the guns on the higher ground, while the crash of war continued on either side.

On the 26th, they were relieved by men of the Yorkshire Light Infantry and moved back to occupy dug-outs once more at Velorenhoek. Now restored to 28th Division, they spent the next few days supplying fatigue parties to their old haunts at Zonnebeke, while a temporary lull ensued in the fighting further north. Clarke describes how things were from the Suffolks' perspective:

Casualties for 24th, 25th and 26th amounting to 334 all told, actually known 29 killed, 150 wounded with 155 missing. Regarding the missing lots were to be seen lying around, impossible to collect all on account of exposure to the Gs. Canadians in a pitiable condition lots being gassed and helpless, could do nothing for them were simply taken back to die, terrible indeed, hanging about like thick yellow mist. The 27th turned out a very quiet day only a few shells dropping our way, one only alighting close by hitting old boarded shed erected for horses ammunition etc. 6294 F Harvey trying to snatch a sleep had laid down by ammunition boxes not 10 minutes previous, shell splintered partition, portion striking Harvey breaking his neck, no sign of wound, had only shaved and cleaned up a short time before, looked well indeed, all signallers very sorry. Day of 28th opened well, weather to match, remained so until close upon 2 pm then the band struck up again, our Dressing Stn being in their way soon gave us the hint to move out of it by dropping a shell upon shed just to our rear, wounding horse belonging to Welsh Regt, next one landing on our roof caused a stir all round, Welsh leaving their trenches and dug-outs which were just in rear of us, all collecting round our unhappy little home (Pilbrough and myself having our quarters with the goat). Had got the range perfect by this time for two or three shells struck well, scattering tiles and bricks etc amongst us thus causing the order to be given to get clear and into any dug-outs round about, but they were apparently waiting for this move, no sooner had the first few men reached the road than another battery started sweeping with shrapnel and concussion, hell of a time for about four hours, lots wounded but few killed, bad cases amongst the wounded, dug-outs having been blown in on them. Lt Woods' arm shattered whilst helping with stretcher, one of the coolest officers that could ever have been to the front, handed stretcher over and proceeded down the road towards Dressing Stn of 85th Brigade. Hard job to remove all wounded but managed it during which time the shelling had slackened considerably. By this time Hdqrs had gathered together just in the village of Valorenhoek, they eventually followed us down causing a scatter amongst the artillery horses, men hung on to them fine, some were terribly wounded, one poor little fellow with horse being completely blown to pieces. Again they found the roof of house under which we had halted, goodness knows what sort of shell it could have been, could scarcely see for fifty yards for brick and tile dust.

Matters were now moving towards the final climax. On 2 May, the Rangers, the Suffolks and the other remnants of the 84th Brigade were sent to dig trenches on the Frezenberg ridge, no more than 2 miles outside the city ramparts, as part of a new defensive line, the Generals having reached the conclusion that a contraction of the present distorted salient was the only practical course. A general withdrawal accordingly took place over the course of two days, being completed in the early hours of 4 May. Although there appears to have been wide agreement that retirement to the new line was the only possible course, a scapegoat was nominated, as is so often the way. Sir Horace Smith-Dorrien, the commander of the Second Army, had long since ceased to enjoy the confidence of the British Commander-in-Chief, Sir John French. The latter chose to find in the retirement further confirmation of his belief that his subordinate lacked the proper offensive spirit. On 6 May, Smith-Dorrien received his marching orders, in somewhat summary fashion, and was replaced by Sir Herbert Plumer.

These things were well above the heads of the rank and file of the 12th Londons. What they knew about was mud, noise, fear and death. With the coming of the better weather, the first had receded somewhat, but the others were ever-present. During the past week the battalion had lost well over a hundred of its members, either killed or injured. For the survivors, their world, which they had enjoyed so carelessly in those happy days of peace, not so many months before, had in a few short weeks contracted into this grim and lethal trap, in which men they had lived and joked with yesterday could today suddenly become mute, inanimate corpses, whose lives had ended amid a confusion of dirt and noise. It was a world represented by an infernal landscape scattered with roofless barns, ruined homesteads and the unburied bodies of men and animals, the air tainted with the acrid smell of chlorine gas, while here and there surviving livestock still roamed, abandoned by their fleeing owners, remote from the conflict yet perilously and bizarrely caught up in it. On 3 May, news reached the men digging their trenches on the ridge that the front-line troops were withdrawing to the new line, obliging them to redouble their efforts throughout the night. By the time dawn was lighting the sky above the eastern ridge, their work was complete and the weary diggers stood to, front-line soldiers themselves once more, waiting and wondering. The enemy artillery had followed the withdrawal and it was not long before it had identified its new targets, causing further casualties in the Rangers' ranks. Four more days went by, as they crouched in their exposed positions (which, contrary to accepted military practice, had been located on the forward slope of the ridge), endured continual shelling and watched the enemy arrive and dig in a few hundred yards away, as part of his preparations for a fresh assault on the now-reduced Salient.

A little further down the line to the right, the Suffolks were similarly placed. Pte Clarke, as a signaller, spent most of his time in the battalion headquarters dug-out with Col. Wallace and others, and later recorded how things fared with them:

...had to form new line of trenches, or a better term for them would be obstacles, for we were no more than such. All of it turned out no good for us, Gs soon found out our move and were soon advancing, could be seen entrenching on early morning of the 3rd, our retirement not taking place until midnight, roughly 400 to 450 yards in front. (Our casualties for our 4 days in dug-outs amounted to 30). Remained rather quiet during 3rd, only one or two casualties, 4th just the opposite, trench-mortars etc continually on the go, 52 casualties out of the 400 men we had left (Sid Binks of Straw Lane being killed). Company of Cheshires arrived to help us at dusk, their Captain named Routh and 4 men being killed with one wounded just after arrival. Our casualties on the 5th amounted to 38, our fellows completely done up, plenty of rain to make things worse. Had been continually on the go from 15th April, Captain Chalmers very often coming back to Hdqrs telling our Colonel what a pitiable condition the men were in and always asking when they were to be relieved, explained to the Colonel about the trenches being one mass of mud and blood. One more company of Cheshires up at night, everything quiet on 6th, no casualties up to 6 pm, from then to 12 noon 7th roughly 30 casualties. We then had 298 men all told, another quiet spell which we were trusting would last until night of 8th when we were to be relieved. The long quietness seemed to suggest something was brewing and it turned out to be so...

It was one hour after midnight on the 8th when, with the expected infantry assault still to take place, the Rangers – though not the Suffolks – found themselves relieved (once more by the 1st Monmouths) and they retired to rest in dug-outs to the south of Wieltje, arriving there at 4 a.m. The pale light of a cold dawn was to offer little respite. At 5.30 a.m. the enemy artillery resumed its attack. Although the Rangers were no longer in the front line, they were scarcely a mile to the rear and by six o'clock shells had found them again, causing further casualties and forbidding all sleep.

The German bombardment was intense and covered a wide area, from the Menin road in an arc round to the place beyond Wieltje which the British had christened 'Mouse Trap Farm'. Not for the first time, the enemy demonstrated his overwhelming superiority in artillery, as the land around declined irrevocably from cultivated farmland to a crater-strewn battlefield. There would be no harvest that year, nor for some years to come.

The British line, being on the forward slope, was in the clear view of the enemy guns, while the ground conditions ordained that the trenches themselves could be no more than three feet deep. The newly-arrived Monmouths, with the Suffolks and the other battalions alongside them, could only endure the shelling and await the

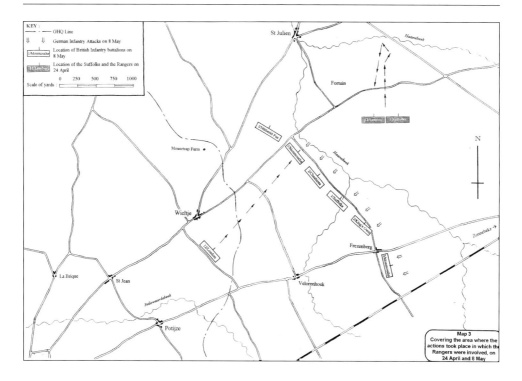

Map 3
Covering the area where the actions took place in which the Rangers were involved, on 24 April and 8 May

now-imminent infantry attack. The first wave appeared at 8.30 a.m. and was stoutly resisted, but, as shelling alternated with further waves, wreaking havoc to the shallow trenches, the casualties mounted, some men being buried as the trench sides collapsed about them, and the attackers began in places to gain the upper hand. With communications to the rear almost completely severed, confusion reigned once more. Some elements of the two battalions dug in on either side of Frezenberg village (the 3rd Monmouths and the 2nd King's Own), believing that they had been sent orders from Brigade to retire, began to do so and the gap thus created gave the Germans their chance to pierce and roll up the British line, already in desperate straits from the five hours of bombardment it had endured. The next battalion to the left (the 1st Suffolks) found its right flank under threat. Beyond the Suffolks lay the 2nd Cheshires, the 1st Monmouths and, on the other side of the Wieltje-Gravenstafel road, the 2nd Northumberland Fusiliers, all unaware of any retirement order and clinging grimly to their positions. Retirement had, in any case, by now become well-nigh impossible through the German fire trained on that lethal slope. Pte Clarke was in the thick of it (being a signaller, he sometimes has recourse to the Morse Code in his diary, seemingly when he wishes an entry to be kept obscure):

> *In dug-out with CO and Adjt working telephone making ready for breakfast but that part of the business did not come off. All remained intact for about 20 minutes when No. 1 dug-out was struck by a shell badly wounding Drew in the head, also burying all rifles etc, causing all there to scatter for the exit, Crabb coming in with me. Our dug-*

out lasted it out about another 10 minutes or so, shell then exploding just in rear of dug-out, knocking telephone me and Crabb out of our positions and wounding Adjt who was directly behind us. Hardly knew what was happening for a few minutes or how we had got off so lucky, telephone, chair, fire all had disappeared, with a hole staring at us a few yards in circumference in their stead. All cleared out to emergency trench which had been dug in rear of ditch and which turned out far worse than all the shattered dug-outs, being up to our waists in water, up to our necks after getting down to it, shells raining all around. During all this they had also dropped one in No.3 dug-out, smashing beam which struck Cpl Pugh, smashing his right leg just above ankle also wounding him in head and left arm. Hottest shop I had ever been in, had just had time to get properly soaked and shaking through with cold when a shell dropped just on edge of trench, burying me with L/C Game, lucky again for after being helped out Game was found to be horribly wounded, having two large holes in back one on either side of backbone. Took him back to No.2 dug-out which had been hit no more and there done him up... Not one of us knew what was happening in front but more or less knew what to expect. Young French 7574 eventually turned up from front line about 11 am being slightly wounded in head, shelling getting wild again causing him to stop with us. He reported our fellows still holding out in trenches men could be seen retiring shortly afterwards to our right (–.–. .–.–. ... – – .– –.) apparently. A few minutes afterwards, Gs appeared to our right so had to get out of trench or would have been enfiladed. Went back or struggled rather on our chests to dug-out with Game, but all the nine of us were in a helpless condition, not a weapon amongst us (Colonel, Sgt Crabb, Brown, French, Manton, Hayward, Humphries (L/C Game wounded) and myself). Colonel at once made the best of things by handing round cigars, had only just managed to get steam up when Gs appeared at the shell hole shouting End-der-oof which apparently meant hands up. Put our hands up and went outside, had only just managed to clear the dug-out when French was shot clean through the heart, direction of shot from Burnt Farm, fell instantly at my feet, a German coming up and placing his cap over his face. Immediately pulled us down amongst them, having to lay then roughly 2 hours in their front line, captured about 11.45 am. During the 2 hours party of King's Own tried to retire, taking place on our left, but simply mad, were mown down like so much corn by Rifle and Machine Gun fire, being only about 80 to 100 yards away. A few that were left put their hands up, 'G's in our line ceased fire immediately, good fellows all round that captured us (77th Hanoverian Regt), kept us from fire as much as possible by making a parapet in our front as well as for themselves, also giving us meat, bread and coffee and doing their best for our wounded. All put in dug-out with Pugh at 1.30 pm, 2 guards remaining with us, their line then advancing towards Ypres. All had the same opinion that they were simply making a walk of it to Ypres then on to Calais finally reaching London. Hardly knew as much as I did, undoubtedly thought that we were all that was left of the Contemptible Little Army.

Meanwhile, back on the British side of the battlefield, the situation was indeed critical. Reinforcements were again urgently needed and reserves were summoned from west of Ypres. These, however, would be some time in arriving; whatever other units which were already in the Salient and which – however tired, however battle-weary, however depleted – were thus more immediately available, had to be thrown in to hold back the enemy, as he threatened to punch right through the British defences. At 11.15 the order came for the 12th Londons to stand to and prepare to advance up to the Frezenberg ridge, whence they had been so recently released, in support of the remnants who were still managing to cling on in their wrecked trenches.

As it happened, the 8th was a Saturday and the sun, by then high in the sky, was announcing a beautiful spring day. Twelve months earlier, that same moment would probably have found young Alfred Hall whitening his cricket boots in preparation for the afternoon's match. Now, that game had been replaced by a much sterner contest in which, with the battalion having already seen so much carnage in its ranks, his expectation of survival that morning cannot have been high. It was 12.45 when they set off, now only some 200 strong – a much diminished band from the 900-odd who had first landed at Le Havre. Further losses were suffered almost immediately, as the battalion was obliged to pass through gaps in the wire of the so-called GHQ line, on which the enemy, as ever holding the high ground, had already trained his machine guns.

Into the cauldron beyond, the dwindling company of Londoners struggled on, led by their officers across ground swept by small-arms fire and amidst shell bursts throwing up high columns of earth mixed with smoke, to the accompaniment of a manic concerto composed of the whistle of arriving missiles, the crash of their explosion and a human chorus of shouts and cries. What few men who remained standing when the trenches were reached dug in there and managed, with other remnants around them, to maintain the semblance of a defence. By their efforts and heavy sacrifice, the German thrust was held and a breakthrough to Ypres and onward to the sea was thwarted. The official History of the Great War judges this attempted counter-attack by the Rangers as 'worthy to rank ... among the historic episodes of the war', while the same source records how a captured British officer, observing the Rangers' advance from the German lines, describes them as coming 'through a barrage of H.E. shells which struck them down by dozens, but they never halted for a minute, and continued to advance until hardly a man remained'. For its part, the Rangers' War Diary recounts the events of that morning in its laconic and unemotional style:

> *11.15 am Order came to go forward and support Monmouths, R of line having been broken by Germans. Battn, about 200 strong, went in following order: A, B, C Coys in first line led by Maj Challon and Maj Foucer, D Coy in support. Machine gun section moving independently on left flank: this section having only one gun.*
> *The whole of the ground from the GHQ trenches to the ridge was being heavily shelled and many casualties occurred before the ridge was reached. The first line crossed the VERLORENHOEK-CHAPEL lane. The second reached same which was under heavy rifle and machine gun fire. About 2.30 pm the Germans occupied the Farm on the lane, which Farm had been HQ of the Cheshire Battn.*

The machine gun was able to reach a point 120 yds behind the front line trenches still held by the Monmouths and from there brought enfilade fire to bear on Germans leaving captured trenches on right and ascending the hill. The gun was subsequently moved about 40 yds to the right rear and was there struck and disabled.

Sgt. Hornell collected stray men, Pioneers and Signallers (about 38 in all) and reported to OC Welsh Regt. Set to convert Dugouts facing YPRES Rd into trenches. Men dropping in brought numbers up to 53.

Rifleman Hall was not among those fifty-three. At some time during the Rangers' gallant advance, he had been slightly wounded and had lost consciousness. When he came to, he seemed to be alone and was, no doubt, somewhat confused. As he stumbled about, he saw, a little way off by the side of one of the streams thereabouts, two figures whom he took to be French soldiers. He started to run down to them, only to find, when it was too late to draw back, that he had mistaken German field-grey for the French *bleu*. Thus he fell into the enemy's hands.

As he was escorted away to captivity, he left a battle which was to rumble on for a further fortnight, finally petering out as the two sides tacitly acknowledged their exhaustion. The Germans could claim to have reduced the Salient to a third of its previous size, while the British, for their part, could take heart from the fact that they had held the line, albeit at heavy cost. Most importantly, the vital Channel ports were still in the possession of the Allies.

The panel on the Menin Gate containing the names of those men of the Rangers who fell in the Ypres Salient, but whose bodies were never found and who thus have no place in any of the cemeteries.

CHAPTER 4

A Kind of Peace

I never heard the details of how my father was transported away from the scene of his capture on Frezenberg ridge and the sounds of battle, into the country of his captors. At about the same time as the Rangers had been struggling up to the ridge, others in the battalions holding the front line whom they were trying to reach, such as the aforementioned H.J. Clarke and his fellow Suffolk man Jack Hayward, were already in German hands. All three were to end up as fellow-prisoners in the same camp. Thus, it is most likely that Hall, taken a few hours later, will have followed the same route as they did and was, indeed, in the same party. Having first been conducted to a suitable assembly point a comfortable distance back from the front line, they were then pushed into railway trucks, offering distinctly primitive conditions and little food, to be borne rapidly eastwards, as Clarke describes:

> *At this time we were taken charge of by Uhlans, settled down about 10 pm at a place called Bacleate, occupied the church which they had made something like a pig-sty, distance about 12 miles from Ypres. Only too glad to get down that night, having to be led by Brown etc for at least 4 miles. Our food consisted of dry bread and water, about 12 noon on Sunday 9th we were supplied with bread and raw bacon with coffee, left by tram for Courtrai, there boarded train, meeting with others who had been captured round about us. Occasional stops with also a brick or two every now and then at fellows who were looking out of the small space we were allowed for air… finally reaching our destination Giessen at 11 pm on night of 10th. Passed a horrible night on the 9th, packed like sardines, sleeping under and over seats such as they were, our food on the 10th consisted of bread, butter and two sausages, which I am sorry to say someone was entitled to more than I was, thus losing my sausages, more coffee but as usual with no milk or sugar. On reaching our Camp we were once more issued with food (bread and water), on the whole we were getting well washed inside. Barracks not at all bad, in fact much better than anyone ever dreamed of. Horrible time until parcels arrived, in all about 5 weeks, fellows looking terribly bad.*

The men of the Suffolks, being regular soldiers, were at least not unfamiliar with the sensations of being ordered off to another country. For the young Londoners of the Rangers, however, who a few short months before had never had occasion to leave their native shores, the transformation to their lives was more disturbing. Almost at a stroke they were finding themselves, in the unfriendliest of circumstances, forcibly translated to a third foreign land, as different from France and Belgium as those latter had been from the familiar homeland in which they had grown up.

Giessen POW camp – a view taken from a window of the camp hospital.

Certainly, for Hall, as for all of them, as he was carried ever further from the rumble of the guns, finding himself in a kind of peace replacing the din and horror of war, speculation concerning the strangeness of his new situation and the shape of his immediate future would be filling his mind. It seemed that, whatever else was to happen, his life was no longer in imminent danger; he was not, after all, destined to be enrolled in those legions whose bones would lie for ever in the Flanders soil. However, his German guards were an ever-present reminder that he was no longer a free man and that, for the immediate future, there was this new experience, captivity, to be endured. But, surely, that could not be for too long – six months, a year at the most, before the war would somehow be brought to an end? It was as well for them all to be spared the knowledge that three and a half years of exile were to pass before they saw home and loved ones again.

Those years of imprisonment would turn out to be a curious mixture of the banal and the everyday, of harshness and frustration, of discomfort and despair, intermixed at times with even a few simple pleasures. They were probably also a time when the normal maturing process, already accentuated and hastened by his experiences on the battlefield, would be given a further thrust. If Alfred Hall was destined to emerge from those years of captivity four years older, he could hardly fail to be both wiser and more hardened to life's vicissitudes.

Meanwhile, back in England, he was for some time officially posted as 'missing'. With the restricted means of communication available in those days, details of who had died and who had survived as prisoners took time to cross the frontier of war. Furthermore, under such conditions and given the heavy casualties being incurred, the only practical method of notifying their families resulted in another stark image of those days: the lists of names which appeared daily in the national newspapers and

The assembled German staff of Giessen POW camp.

which were anxiously scrutinised in search of a particular name and the fate of its owner. In later years, my mother often recalled those troubled weeks, when she paid many visits to the War Office in London, where the official lists were available for consultation by the public.

The prisoner of war camp to which Clarke, Hall and other survivors from the fighting were taken was situated on a hill near some pinewoods about a mile and a half outside the town of Giessen, some 30 miles due north of Frankfurt, and consisted mainly of rows of wooden huts, raised some two to three feet off the ground. Each hut was equipped with wooden bedsteads and straw mattresses and was heated by a number of stoves. Neither fuel nor food was plentiful, but conditions improved somewhat as the war went on. In those early days, the population was mostly French, but as time passed the numbers of the British inmates gradually increased.

Numerous films and books, derived from the Second World War in particular, have made us familiar with images of POWs, imprisoned in their wire compounds and, deprived both of their liberty and of outlets for their latent energy, devising various means of occupying their leisure hours. Apart from attempts at escaping, sport and theatrical entertainments are shown as figuring prominently. A quarter of a century earlier it had been much the same. On 20 July 1915, a cricket match took place at Giessen, between 'Nobby Clarke's XI' and 'Nobby Hall's XI', the scorebook consisting of two pages in the former's diary. At that time, proper playing equipment must have been sparse, and one imagines that some resource will have been needed to compensate for this. Clarke's team, batting first, made 48, thanks to a useful 20

The programme for the 'Giessen Variétés', produced on 25 July 1915.

runs from one Cummings. In reply, Hall's XI could muster no more than 16, though the captain could console himself with having taken 5 wickets.

Five days later, an evening's entertainment, called the 'Giessen Variétés', was organised, with a bill long enough to keep the audience entertained for hours. Given the camp population at that time, it was a mainly French enterprise, and what the British prisoners in the audience made of much of it must be the subject of conjecture. However, Hall, at number 8 on the bill, 'In his songs', saw to it that *les anglais* were at least represented, as did one or two others among his compatriots. They were learning to make the best of it.

For all that, their situation left much to be desired. By 1915, various reports suggesting ill-treatment and hardship in the enemy's prison camps had filtered through to the British side, giving rise to much disquiet, both amongst the public and in official quarters, about the well-being of the considerable numbers of British soldiers now being held prisoner by the enemy. With a view to investigating this question and alleviating it if necessary, the British government set up a 'Committee

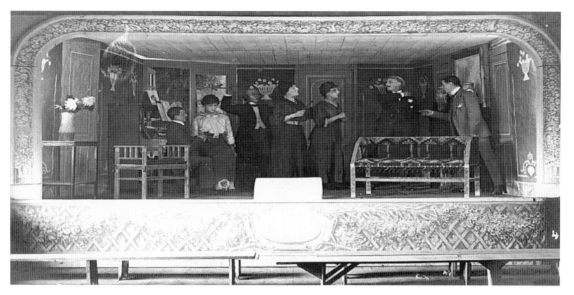

A scene from a play staged by the French prisoners at Giessen. All the props, costumes, etc. were made in the camp by the prisoners themselves.

Sgt Hardwick, a Canadian POW, who was consulted by Dr Ohnesorg. He acted as chaplain to the Protestant prisoners at Giessen, having been given permission to undertake these duties by the Bishop of Montreal.

53

on the Treatment by the Enemy of British Prisoners of War'. On an international basis, but inspired by the same general theme, agreements were arrived at for inspections of all the combatant nations' POW camps to be carried out from time to time by representatives of disinterested parties, such as the International Red Cross and certain neutral nations. This, the British hoped, would reveal to them whether some of the more alarming reports were true or false and would also ensure that the treatment of the prisoners and their living conditions were in accordance with the Hague Convention and with reasonable standards of civilised behaviour. One such visit of inspection was made to Giessen on 15 December 1915 by the American Assistant Naval Attaché in Berlin, Dr Ohnesorg. His report, sent to the American Ambassador in London, Walter Hines Page, and passed on to the Foreign Office, contains some description, albeit from a visiting outsider – and one who was not allowed unrestricted access – of the conditions at Giessen around that time:

The afternoon of this day (15.12.15) Mr Osborne and I visited the camp at Giessen. Thirteen Hundred and seventy five (1375) British prisoners of war are confined in the camp and six hundred and one (601) attached to the camp are at work on the surrounding country.

There is a great deal of friction between the German authorities and the British prisoners of war over the question of work and numerous complaints were made regarding the treatment which men received at working camps. At least two gave details of being struck by a German soldier or civilian. They are employed in agricultural work, various industries, foundries and rolling mills, mines, quarries, etc. I had a long talk with Sergt. Hardwick of the Royal Montreal Infantry, who acts as chaplain of the Camp. He was convinced that there were some cases of ill-treatment and he also said that he thought that frequently some of the men, by their demeanour and actions, courted trouble.

Those of the British prisoners who were in the camp were lined up and a critical inspection of their clothing, etc. made. A very large majority were without overcoats, a great number without suitable shoes and many without underclothing and socks. They stated that their names had been noted several times in regard to clothes needed but that nothing had come of it, and that in general it was impossible to obtain clothes upon application to the German authorities. The majority of them were in uniform, but many were in civilian clothes or in parts of French uniforms. All of their clothing was shabby and their own uniforms had been decorated by the Germans with a red strip along the outer surface of the arms and with a broad one down the middle of the back. This had been done by the former commandant because the British uniform in cut and color resembled the 'Sport-Anzug' worn by many Germans.

A visit was made to the camp hospital, and the British sick and wounded seen.

A Canadian soldier has been in the Arrestanstalt of the Garrison since August last, awaiting trial by Court Martial for assaulting a German soldier. We were refused permission to see him. The six men tried by Court Martial at Friedburg were interned at this camp. Seven men belonging to the camp are imprisoned at Butzbach, awaiting trial for refusing to work.

A newly instituted 'helping committee' made up of members of the interned was met with here, and also in the camp at Limburg. This is an admirable idea and does much good among the prisoners of war. Each nationality had such a committee which interests itself in the welfare of those of their comrades who need help.

Dr Ohnesorg refers to POWs who were sent out of the camp to work. Under the terms of the Hague Convention, all non-commissioned POWs could, within certain limits, be made to work by their captors. For this purpose, those in Germany were organised into units called *Kommandos*, where they not only worked but also lived on site. In August 1915, some months before Dr Ohnesorg's visit, a number of prisoners, amongst them Alfred Hall and the Suffolk men Clarke and Hayward, became thus employed, when they were sent away from Giessen to work as farm labourers. The village to which they were all sent was called Mensfelden, about 30 miles to the west, near the town of Limburg-an-der-Lahn, in the handsome rolling country of the Lahn valley. From its relatively elevated position, the views from the village stretch away to the south as far as the hills of the Taunus, while in the opposite direction the land undulates similarly to an horizon formed by the Westerwald. Altogether a not unattractive location to spend one's days, the modern visitor might feel, as he strolls along the peaceful streets, admiring the well-kept white-walled houses and enjoying glimpses of the fields and wooded downs which form the surrounding countryside. Eighty-odd years ago, however, the reality was of a different order. Work on the land, unassisted by modern mechanical aids, was hard labour and – so far as the prisoners were concerned – cheap labour, exacted from men held against their will on enemy soil and forced to work for long hours for the profit of an alien master. Inevitably, relations between the farmers and their captive labourers were coloured by the frustration and resentment felt by the latter at the position into which they had been thrust. Matters were not helped by the fact that few, if any, of the prisoners would have had any previous opportunity to visit Germany and to gain a closer understanding of its people and their way of life, while perhaps even fewer of their 'hosts' can have acquired much useful knowledge of the people of that far-off island across the North Sea. The situation was not one to encourage ready friendships. To Alfred Hall, being town-bred and brought up to office work rather than manual labour, life was one of unfamiliar and uncongenial toil, assisting his nation's enemies and rewarded by a pittance, in a foreign land where the contrasts between the local customs and working practices and those in his own country were much greater than they are today. Furthermore, his work contract was of an utterly uncertain length, its ending being completely outside his control. No question of handing in his notice and looking for something more suitable!

The British prisoners' sleeping quarters were in what was in normal times the *Turnhalle*, or the village gymnasium, and which they called their barracks, while the French prisoners who had been sent to work alongside them at Mensfelden were housed separately in the *Gasthaus* – the village inn.

Neustrasse

Gruss aus Mensfelden

Two postcards from those days, with contemporary views of the village of Mensfelden.

Mensfelden   Totalansicht.

Partie an der Post.

Partie an der Schule.

Jack Hayward, of the 1st Suffolks, at Mensfelden in October 1915.

Gaston Chevallier, of the 76e Régiment d'Infanterie, with 'his' oxen. This picture illustrates one of the differences between German and British agriculture in those days: British farmers tended to use horses.

Rfn Arthur Lapworth and Rfn Alfred Hall proceeding with the farmer's horse at MENSFELDEN, Germany

Left: Erstwhile Riflemen Arthur Lapworth and Alfred Hall, both lately in the ranks of the 12th County of London Regiment, at Mensfelden in August 1915, accompanied by the farmer's horse.
Right: Hall, photographed outside the barracks in December 1915, wearing 'our coat' – so called because it was at that time the only one they could muster between them.

Once arrived at Mensfelden, Alfred Hall, like his fellow-prisoner 'Nobby' Clarke, resolved to keep a diary. For the next two and a half years, he filled two small pocket books with his thoughts, his fears, his hopes and his frustrations, through good days and bad. The books also served as general notebooks, in which he meticulously recorded such information as the names and home addresses of the others sharing his life at Mensfelden and of the numerous benevolent people at home – many of them complete strangers – who sent them food parcels. One other name he added to his list, with an address much closer at hand. This was a certain Lieber, the farmer to whom he had been assigned and with whom he was to have an unhappy, not to say stormy relationship:

Tuesday, Sept 14th 1915
The worst job of the lot. Potato digging. Filled 23 sacks this morning, then it rained like mad. L. and I took cover behind one sack, till I knocked it over. Lieber swore. Reached the house wet through, changed into a suit belonging to August (pronounced Owhoost). Looked a guy.

The assembled POWs, mostly British with a few French and accompanied by their guards, in November 1915. Alfred Hall is seated on the musician's right.

> *Wednesday, Sept 15th 1915 to Saturday, Sept 25th 1915*
> *Spuds Spuds Spuds. Fed up with 'em, metaphorically or otherwise.*
> *On Sept 22 Holland (Canadian) escaped, reported capture on Sept 24th.*
> *Lucky week. Parcel from Con, Harry Hulcoop, Miss Paget, Lady Dodds.*

Hall is noncommittal about Holland's escape attempt. Clarke is more forthright:

> *22/9/15*
> *Holland of the Canadians made a fool of himself by trying to escape, roughly 40 hours before being caught, had managed to wander nearly 4 kilometres during that time being found in the very next village (Obermesen).*

Life on the farm went on. For Hall there were frustrating moments, as relations with his master declined:

> *October 1st 1915*
> *Row with Lieber this morning on spud field. Threatened to go back to Giessen. I expect he threatened me.*

> *A small incident hardly worth recording occurred on Oct 17th 1915 at Mensfelden Germany where I am employed as Farmers labourer by my employer (Humph 3d per*

Leonard Dummer, with his horse, in 1916. Dummer served in the King's Own Royal Lancaster Regiment.

day). Considered I should work Sunday morning. I objected and stayed in barrack. He kicked up awful shindy so I wouldn't go to the house for any meals that day (Sunday). Monday morning came and Lieber and I had a norful row. He yelled at me and I at him. The gist of it all was that if I didn't come in on Sundays he would send me back to Giessen. I told him I didn't care a tuppenny damn where I was in this infernal country. Whereupon seeing I was indifferent he sobered down and the following week passed in comparative silence and on Saturday 23rd October Mrs Guy cried and asked me to come in on the Sunday. I agreed (she only cried for the work).

'Mrs Guy' is presumably Frau Lieber. Hall was not the only prisoner to find himself in conflict with his employer:

November 15th 1915
J. Land and farmer and engineer rowed. Land struck both men the engineer took up hammer at Jimmy (just like this infernal squareheaded 84 round the waist nation). J. narrowly escaped court-martial. Anyhow so far (18/11/15) nothing has been heard further of the matter.

Wednesday, November 17th 1915
Photo taken with Lieber and crowd. 'Spect I look a guy as usual. Just a few words about

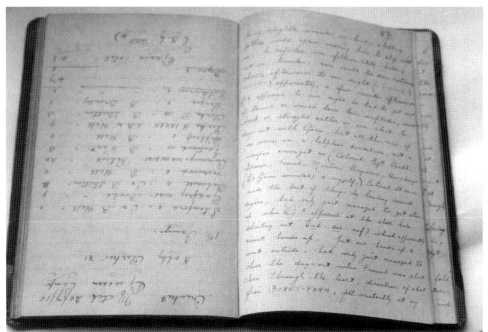

The diary kept by 'Nobby' Clarke.

The two notebooks in which Alfred Hall kept his diary.

The farmhouse occupied by the Schwenk family (see page 105).

> *my honoured employer and family. Herr Lieber is a man of 55 years of age. Small in height but remarkably strong for his age and size. His one god is money. To obtain this, owing to the primitive methods employed, it necessitates hard work, devilish hard work. He doesn't mind that tho', revels in work and dirt, especially the latter. Have never met a filthier illmannered race of people than Germans. Frau Lieber and daughter are just as bad.*

Thus, from the sentiments expressed, the reader cannot have failed to note that Alfred Hall had at that time little love for the German race. His was certainly a very widespread attitude amongst the British in those days – reciprocated, one should add, by the German people's view of the British. All very deplorable, many today might say, from the high-minded standpoint which the long years of peace have allowed us to adopt and with the notion of a single, united European state so much in the air. But such were the popular attitudes in those very different and less fortunate times. As has already been observed, only a small minority was given the opportunity to venture beyond their native land and any regard on the part of the people of one nation for those of another would be a tender plant, prone to wither in the frosts created by international disputes – a phenomenon which even today, perhaps, is not entirely unknown.

In the yard of another Mensfelden farmhouse, a French prisoner minds the carthorse, while his stout German guard stands by.

Furthermore, like all his companions, my father had but recently come from battlefields where he had seen many of his comrades killed or maimed in conflict with those same Germans. War, by its nature, is hardly calculated to engender a spirit of peaceful international brotherhood. Added to this, many and widespread were the stories of alleged German atrocities which were in circulation then and throughout the war. With the passage of the years, some of the worst have been shown to be imaginary, though others still stand, apparently true. At the time, all were believed. On 7 May, the day before his capture, the Cunard liner *Lusitania* had been sunk off Ireland by a U-boat, with the loss of over 1,000 lives, including many women and children. Numerous other liners and merchant ships were to suffer the same fate and such incidents naturally stirred strong emotions in the population as a whole. At Ypres, two weeks earlier, the Germans had been the first to use cylinder gas, which contravened the rules of warfare and tended to be regarded then by the British as further evidence of German 'frightfulness' – to use a word which was much in vogue at the time. (Although, later on, driven by the exigencies of 'total war', Britain overcame her scruples and made use of the new weapon herself.) Other stories which aroused much anger in Great Britain were those concerning the harsh treatment meted out to the conquered Belgians by the

The two houses as they look today.

November 1915: Prisoner Hall is holding the horse's head, 'looking a guy as usual'. Sitting in the cart is Herr Lieber.

German occupying forces, including the shooting of members of the civilian population. Finally, reports of alleged brutal behaviour by German guards towards Allied prisoners were many, constituting one of the specific reasons which had caused the British government to set up the 'Committee on the Treatment by the Enemy of British Prisoners of War', referred to earlier. This committee sat throughout the war and in the latter stages was responsible for the interviewing of returned prisoners – who had either escaped or had been repatriated as unfit for military service, under a two-way arrangement agreed at The Hague in 1917. The accounts given by these men naturally varied, dependent on their personal experiences. While no small number were able to relate examples of enemy soldiers, medical orderlies and others who performed various acts of kindness towards POWs, particularly the wounded, there was also no shortage of those who told of incidents alleging conduct by their captors which ranged from poor medical attention, through physical assault, to unlawful killing. My father himself, shortly after his capture, witnessed the shooting dead of a British prisoner, Skinner by name, apparently for nothing worse than insolence. (In fairness, it should here be acknowledged that the shooting of prisoners on the battlefield, though reprehensible, did take place and was not limited to the German side only.)

PROCLAMATION

A l'avenir les localités situées près de l'endroit où a eu lieu la destruction des chemins de fer et lignes télégraphiques seront punies sans pitié (il n'importe qu'elles soient coupables ou non de ces actes.) Dans ce but des otages ont été pris dans toutes les localités situées près des chemins de fer qui sont menacés de pareilles attaques. et au premier attentat à la destruction des lignes de chemins de fer, de lignes télégraphiques ou lignes téléphoniques, ils seront immédiatement fusillés

Bruxelles, le 5 Octobre 1914

Le Gouverneur

VON DER GOLTZ

PROCLAMATION.

In future the inhabitants of places situated near railways and telegraph lines which have been destroyed will be punished without mercy (whether they are guilty of this destruction or not) For this purpose, hostages have been taken in all places in the vicinity of railways in danger of similar attacks, and at the first attempt to destroy any railway. telegraph, or telephone line. they will be shot immediately.

Brussels. 5th October. 1914

The Governor,

VON DER GOLTZ

One of many proclamations which were posted in Belgium by the occupying power.

All these matters served only to exacerbate the generally prevailing antipathy felt towards Germans in general, which was clearly shared by my father. Later on in his imprisonment, as we shall see, he undoubtedly modified his views, as he met other Germans, civilians mainly, whom he found as good-natured and amiable as any of his own kind. For the time, however, he was constrained in an alien land, far from the familiar warmth of the life he had known, separated from the family, fiancée and friends he had left behind, and forced to work at hard and unfamiliar labour for little reward, under a stern and hostile master. And there seemed to be no sign of an end:

January 10th 1916
I'm going to grouse. Fact! When is the war going to end. I have been awfully patient but I'm anxious terribly anxious to get back to civilization. Never dreamt I'd be in this cultured? (Big query) country so long.

Any contact with home was a welcome shaft of light through the gloom:

January 14th 1916
Was rather pleased and surprised to see an old man come to Mensfelden. He had been in England for 37 years at Torquay. Speaking excellent English had only left England on 14/11/15. Was pleased to know everybody in the Old Country was happy and everything as usual.

Arthur Lapworth, with the Lieber family.

Three more of the French POWs who were also employed on the local farms at Mensfelden.

Above: Jules Druse, of the 16e Chasseurs à pied. To the village children, these strangers, nominally their enemies and speaking more than one unfamiliar tongue, must have been a source of great interest.

A quartet of French prisoners, with a fascinated gaggle of children looking on.

Left: Caporal Pierre Ferrié of the 80e Régiment d'Infanterie. Right: Georges Dron of the 402e Régiment de ligne.

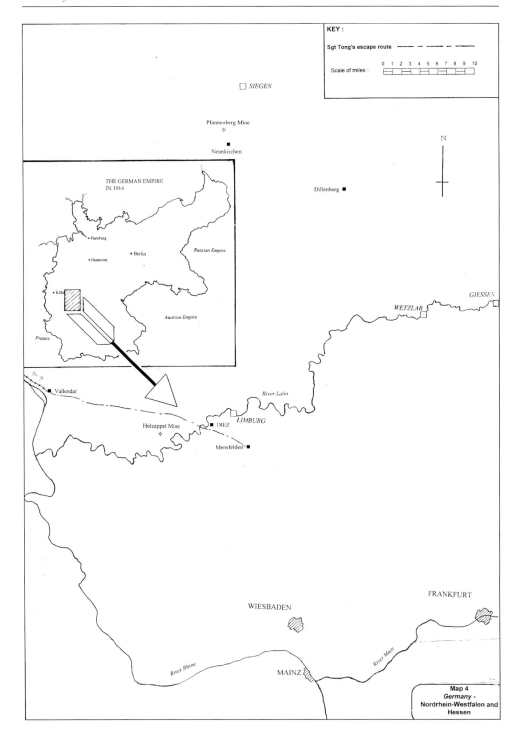

KEY :

Sgt Tong's escape route

Scale of miles : 0 1 2 3 4 5 6 7 8 9 10

SIEGEN

N

Pfannenberg Mine

Neunkirchen

Dillenburg

THE GERMAN EMPIRE
IN 1914

Hamburg

Berlin

Hannover

Russian Empire

Köln

Austrian Empire

France

GIESSEN

WETZLAR

River Lahn

Vallendar

LIMBURG

Holzappel Mine

DIEZ

Mensfelden

WIESBADEN

FRANKFURT

River Rhine

MAINZ

River Main

Map 4
Germany -
**Nordrhein-Westfalen and
Hessen**

January 25th 1916

Lieber's outburst of rage and hatred re the war and especially my remark of 1920 and the blockade. He will not send me back to Giessen but is keen on getting me in S.B. whereas I intend to beat him if I can.

February 19th 1916

One year ago today I was in hospital. As last year, it is raining cats and dogs. God help the poor fellows in the trenches, I've had some. Am of opinion the war will last till October next. This country is remarkably economical but I think and sincerely hope will go to the wall. I visit Sergt. Tong who is in bed with his wound (can't see how he could be anywhere without it). Glad he is getting better. A good Frau. Tomorrow is Sunday. How I look forward to that day. Yesterday Mother's Xmas parcel arrived. Holy Smoke! It had been through the mill some. I rescued from the debris Xmas pudding gloves and biscuits. Arrival also of Birthday parcel in good condish. Gee! Some cake. Reminded me of last year's cake. Will upschneider morgen mittag. From the German papers gather there is some terribly heavy fighting going on at Ypres and in France. Of course they (the Gs) have obtained huge successes. Would give all I possess for a copy of the 'Times'. Boots are letting in the water. Am wondering how to overcome this difficulty. Must go and feed the cows. Au revoir diary!

The parcels receiving yard at Giessen. Prisoners of several nationalities are assembled for – so far as the lucky ones are concerned – some of the happier moments of their captivity.

On receipt, the parcels must be taken to the 'Censor's Room' for examination, before their respective owners are able to enjoy their contents.

The arrival (or absence) of food parcels bulked very large in all prisoners' minds. Apart from those sent by the Red Cross, many parcels came from private sources, such as relatives and friends of the prisoners, as well as from other organisations, set up for the purpose by private individuals (such as Lady Dodds, mentioned earlier), anxious to make their contribution to the national war effort. Some of the parcels seemed to 'go astray', giving rise to dark suspicions at the British end. One minute in a Foreign Office file on the subject sardonically remarked: 'Yes. Of course it is quite easy for the Germans to invoke bad packing of parcels as an excuse for the non-arrival of their contents. For all we know, any amount of petty larceny may be going on.'

On the other hand, it was inevitable that some privately sent parcels should be inadequately packed for their rather arduous journey (note that his 'Christmas' parcel eventually arrived nearly two months late and in poor condition) and in 1915 the GPO had been constrained to issue advice to the public: 'Communication with Prisoners of War Interned Abroad'. In advising that parcels should be very strongly packed, it made the following suggestions:

> Strong double cardboard or strawboard boxes, corrugated being most suitable,
> Tin boxes (i.e. biscuit tins),
> Strong wooden boxes,
> Several folds of stout packing paper.

This smart pair were just two of the many Russian prisoners who were also employed in the area.

Arthur Lapworth, photographed here in February 1916, was my father's closest friend amongst the prisoners, being also from the 12th Londons and captured on the same day, 8 May 1915.

A modern view of the village of Mensfelden. The old Turnhalle *building still stands and lies on the other side of the road from the white-walled house, near the bottom centre-left. Hehnerstrasse runs through the village from right to left across the centre of the picture.*

Mensfelden 1995

Between whiles, Alfred Hall is still watching the war as best he can and, like everyone else, hoping for its end:

March 6th 1916
I read in the G. Papers that a German ship has sunk many English ships in the Atlantic. Must get full particulars when (Oh shut up).

March 20th 1916
I understand there is some very heavy fighting in France along the whole front. Does this mean the end of the war.

Nearly a year in captivity now and the frustration and restiveness is growing. Twenty-five years old – life is slipping past. At least he was spared the knowledge that it was yet to last for the better part of three more years.

March 28th 1916
Arrival last Friday at Mensfelden a new man. One of Kitchener's Army. Captured on Feb 19 '16 at the Cemetery. Was peppered with questions by we fellows. Arthur asked him if he had come across a place called England during his travels. Have been wondering why they haven't sent that Song Book. Although there are only 17 of us here we must try and get up some sort of a concert for Easter and we all know each others songs off by heart. Connie's and Elsie's photograph came but it is not at all good. Con looks frightfully old. Have at present got the best collection of photos and PCs in the Barrack. On the 22nd of this month ended the subscription for the German War Loan (the 4th) which amounted to 10 Milliarden Mark (about £500,000,000). This village (Mensfelden) subscribed over 100,000 Marks (about £5000) including 19,000 Marks from the school children. This amount of course was given them by their parents. Although there is the usual amount of patriotism yet it is certain that this village at least lent their money to the G. Govt. only for the greed of gain, viz: 5% interest.

More trouble flared up between prisoners and captors:

April 1st 1916
Jerry Court strikes.

April 3rd 1916
Jerry returns to Giessen. Very sorry as I liked him immensely. He left me a note which tells its own tale and which I copy here:

Dear Nobby
Just a line hoping it won't break your heart which old Brick Dust tried to break mine. He came back this morning saying they telephoned through to say I must work. I said 'No' and he started knocking me about with his rifle about 12 times. He put me in the

fire shed for 5 minutes and brought me back. I leave my kind regards to all the boys.
Your old chum
Jerry
Poor Old Jerry.

April 13th 1916

According to the German papers they (the Gs) are having it all their own way in France,
I should like to know a little of the truth anyhow. Am pleased to know Connie is
learning the piano.

May 27th 1916

It's a long time since I contributed anything to this so-called diary owing to the busy
time I have been having working from 6.30 am to 9 pm, and on the go from early
morning to late evening with a few short lapses for meals. 15-20 minutes breakfast
20-30 minutes dinner and 15-20 minutes afternoon coffee. Of course I must
remember I am a prisoner of war and these people can do with me as they like. BUT
Alfred wasn't born yesterday. 'Nuff said. Last Thursday week Allen returned to
Giessen, poisoned blood. We are getting very short of Englishmen at Mensfelden.
Last August there were 42. At present the number is 14, and Frenchmen over 40.
We have been having very hot weather recently and one feels it especially in the fields
ploughing harrowing rolling sowing. Continually walking, walking. Thistle snatching
is a tedious job. I must say I am in very good health but Heaven knows what we
POWs would look like if it was not for our parcels from England. Yet I think we
should consider ourselves lucky in working on a farm. A man could not possibly live
in a Lager 6 months without parcels from home, and I <u>absolutely refuse</u> to work
elsewhere than at those occupations agreed upon at the Hague Convention. The state
of this country is awful, I cannot imagine how the poorer classes in the towns are
existing. They are short of everything. The farmers are of course better off than any.
Butter is 2/4 a pound, the smallest price for meat is 2/2 a pound and all other neces-
sities are proportionately dear. One must bear in mind that in peacetime the prices of
all articles are very much cheaper than in England because the people are content to
work for a very small wage. Also, a woman in Germany whose husband is at the
front and who has three children receives from the Govt. only 36 Marks a month.
The poorer classes in the towns must exist entirely on the infamous black bread and
pigs' fat. A few weeks ago the G. Govt. monopolized all the copper kettles, boilers
etc. They intend to hang out. I heard a remark the other day to the effect that the
speaker considered the Germans very plucky in holding out so long, to which I replied
that it was easy for those in authority here to herald themselves as the criterion of
pluck and courage when the shortage of food supplies does not affect their own huge
paunches. <u>Tomorrow is Sunday</u>.

May 30th 1916

I cannot understand why I am getting no letters. Have received 1 in 2 weeks and that
from Connie. Forgotten? No, I think not. Makes the time go quicker when a few letters

turn up. Great deal in these papers about peace conferences, etc. All paper talk I believe. Must go and see to those bloomin' old cows now. Au revoir.

June 10th 1916
Lamb's Essays and Letters. Most delightful. Lamb lived in Colebrook Row Islington and his house still stands. New River at the rear 6 rooms.

Whit Monday, June 12th 1916
Bad news always seems to come with a terrible rush. A terrible awful crushing and annihilating defeat of ENGLISH (I quote the German papers) in the North Sea and worse than all the tragic death of the soldiers' idol L.K. I have heard that he is not dead. God grant that this is true. I suppose I must say 'naturally' the Gs are in high glee. Au revoir my holiday. Hardest work of all to come in July and August. How I hate it all.

The above refers of course to the Battle of Jutland, which was fought on 31 May. This report, together with that of the death of Lord Kitchener (L.K.), illustrates another aspect of the frustration suffered by POWs, particularly those away from the main camps. What news of the progress of the war they could get was largely confined to the German newspapers – whose versions of events could hardly to be expected to show them in a light favourable to the Allied cause (not to mention the language difficulty, though this particular English reader will by now have begun to acquire some knowledge of German).

June 22nd 1916
Allen returns from Giessen. Seemingly they get more news there than we do here. A few English papers filter through somehow. How I do hate this life here, but my hatred of the life cannot be compared with my hatred of the people especially the military. Oh there will be a few debts to pay when the war is over. Brickdust, that <u>thing</u> that patrols the streets as a man and tries to break our spirits. (He could never do it in a year of Sundays). The four men shot (2 English, 2 French) for refusing to work in munitions factory. Others bayonetted and bruised for minor 'offences'. How I do love my hatred and what a joy it will be when I can wipe a few items off a full slate. What a grand beautiful massacre there'll be when English POWs meet Gs on level ground.

His continued frustration is making him unduly bloodthirsty! 'Brickdust' is undoubtedly their German guard.

July 5th 1916
Great English offensive. Lam it into 'em boys. G papers say that all English attacks have been driven back.

Some limited news of the Battle of the Somme has filtered through. Later the same day, a second entry muses on more personal matters:

July 5th 1916
It has often occurred to me that many questions I ask in my letters home are not answered. I wonder why for instance whether Mother is still sacking that 13/- per week for me. George's regt No etc. Whether Billy Curtis has visited home yet etc etc.

The remainder of that second summer of captivity passed by, unmarked by any entries in the diary, possibly due to lack of time – or energy – after long hours spent in the fields. With the approach of autumn, the diary resumes its place in the prisoner's life:

September 16th 1916
I fall down the barn and am wounded yet must work. What a life! The last G War Loan is now being subscribed. How much? Hope old George does not have to go back to France.

September 27th 1916
Letter from Galicia to say Wilhelm has been killed on 17th inst. Killed instantly. Only 2 days in trenches.

Left: H.J. 'Nobby' Clarke, of the 1st Suffolk Regiment, captured on Frezenberg Ridge on the same day as 'Nobby' Hall and, like him, a cricketer and a diarist.
Right: J.W. Hayward, also of the 1st Suffolks, at Mensfelden on 3 March 1916. This was 'Jack', owner and player of the mandolin.

Sunday, Oct 1st 1916
Jack is playing his mandoline (Silver threads among the gold) sitting at the head of his
bed. I am at the foot having just finished my letter (tune has changed to the 'Rosary').
Have a bad toothache and will go to bed. My favourite song 'Afton Water' now. Oh
Olive how I can see you every time I sing that tune which is many times a day, yet
what a change I am expecting to see when I get home.

In those days, the tradition of home entertainment was still strong. Some years
were yet to pass after the ending of the war before it began to die, first with the
arrival of radio, followed later by that of the record player and finally television. But,
before those later times, there was usually no shortage of those who were versed and
who took pleasure in contributing, with voice or instrument, to the entertainment
of the assembled company. Thus, in the evenings in the barracks at Mensfelden, the
solace of music was always available, sometimes stirring memories of happier times
back home.

Olive was my father's youngest sister, whilst George was his elder brother.

Monday, October 2nd 1916
Tonight at 7.30 pm L. required me to unload 80 sacks of potatoes. Good Heavens!
Am I a machine as well as a prisoner. I refused of course.

Tuesday, October 3rd 1916
At 6.45 am I am in fields potato digging. I finish at 7 pm. Meal times amount to 40
mins. Query? Am I too tired, fed up, anything you care to call it, to write in this book.
Oh! For a return to civilization.

Saturday, October 7th 1916
I write in bed, after a sleepless night (Neuralgia). Many attempts have been made to
get me to work, but I am obstinate. I consign them all to a warmer place than this
planet, hang 'em. Leave me alone, that's all I ask.

Tuesday, October 10th 1916
Whilst Arthur was in Limburg today with a load of potatoes a child about 4 years old
asked him for 1 pfennig (1/10 of a penny). Arthur replied that he hadn't one
whereupon this poor offspring of a starving, downtrodden military requested a piece of
bread (God help the children).

October 16th 1916
Allen and I have teeth out at Lucks. (Unlucky day).

October 17th 1916
I am not in training for a walk round the world but today (had I a speedometer attached
to my feet it would have registered about 50 miles) – I have harrowed and harrowed till
I'm sure there are harrows on my brain.

Spuds, I must refer to this again. We live on 'em, work on 'em, speak of 'em and dream of 'em. The whole German race at present seem to be existing entirely on 'em. The Lieber family consume about 20 lbs at one meal. They don't eat 'em. They simply absorb 'em.

October 19th 1916
Olive's photo arrives. What a dear flapper it is.

October 27th 1916
I have two more teeth out and am not likely to forget the experience. A little rest now will be greatly appreciated.

November 4th 1916
Am feeling better in health. Just before leaving the house to sow a field of wheat, the old lady required consoling as per usual on account of her son. This fell to my lot this time. Next time I hope somebody else is in the house. Arthur is ill. What a life. Parcels are very conspicuous by their absence.

Monday, Nov 6th 1916
Arthur returns to Giessen amid much sorrowful adieus. Fortunately he is expected to

Pausing in his hay-raking, the prisoner on the left (distinguished by the stripe down his trousers) was one Chamberlain, of the 9th Battalion, 1st Canadian Contingent.

return here in 2 or 3 weeks. I go with him to the station and was surrounded by all sorts and conditions of men women and children and we are subjected to a lot of criticism and remarks, as we had our military blue greatcoats and WHITE gloves. Poor chap, he looked pretty sad.

Sunday, November 19th 1916
Have been having a freezing time in the fields this past week, which was compensated by a goodly supply of parcels. Letters and parcels are a good thing. One is inclined to turn the other cheek to the smiter the moment they arrive. Here come the rabble and I cannot write with this crowd around me.

Parcels, whilst constituting a link with home and a reminder that they were not forgotten, were more materially a well-nigh essential addition to their meagre official rations. By this point in the war, the Royal Navy blockade of German ports had resulted in serious food shortages throughout Germany from which, understandably, the prisoners suffered to at least the same extent as everyone else – though, as the diary observed earlier, on farms the effects of the food shortages were probably mitigated.

November 25th 1916
Arthur returns from Giessen of which I am well pleased. He brings much interesting news. Logan of the Kings Own has been killed by one of the guards by a bayonet thrust for some paltry offence. Moreton of the 12th London Regt. died in hospital at Giessen. He was seriously wounded at Ypres on 8/5/15 and at Giessen his left leg was amputated at the thigh, but the job was bodged for after a while the bone protruded through the skin and another piece of bone was taken off. This was again unsuccessful and again was a like operation performed. Before he was thoroughly well again he was taken for a hot bath, placed in the bath and forgotten for $1\frac{1}{2}$ hours. He contracted cramp in the bath, was unable to move. The water, of course, got cold and – he died.
KULTURED COUNTRY THIS.

November 29th 1916
I receive 3 letters and I feel happy. One is from Connie one from Elsie and one from Mrs Atkinson. Being near Xmas they herald the approach of something good. My 3rd Xmas away from the Old Country and <u>the last</u> unless I'm unlucky.

Connie is his fiancée (later my mother) and Elsie is his second sister. As for his hopes for peace in 1917, not only were they to be dashed, but that year was to see the lowest point of his fortunes during his captivity. Indeed, the benevolent mood manifested in the last entry was to be of the shortest possible duration:

November 30th 1916
Am not in a good temper. Could coolly shoot the whole family today.

Or, in English, Christmas 1916. The building on the left is their home, the Turnhalle.

December 16th 1916

Peace and rumours of peace!!

For the last 2 days the papers have been full of reports of peace meetings in the Reichstag. The K. always a paragon of that which is good and God's left-hand man, has asked the Allied powers to come to some agreement. There is a great deal of bluff in the note and a keen desire to shift the blame off his own shoulders to those in England. Rumour hath it today that England will not have peace yet and 'Gott strafe Englands' are filling the air even more than previously. We shall see what we shall see.

Through the year 1916, the US President, Woodrow Wilson, had made more than one effort to encourage the Allies and the Central Powers to enter into peace negotiations, but with not the slightest success. At the end of the year, as the diary implies, Germany and Austria made a move of their own by issuing, through the Americans, a Diplomatic Note containing proposals for ending the fighting. But at that stage neither side felt itself so weakened that it was prepared to make the necessary concessions. Both were still hoping to land the knock-out blow, with the fight set to continue for many more bloody rounds while, for their part, the prisoners of Mensfelden would have to remain in their unnatural detention for many more long months.

Meanwhile, they must make the best of it. Whether a concert took place at Easter, as my father had hoped, is not recorded, but the maintenance of morale demanded that another Christmas could not be allowed to pass without the effort being made and preparations were put in hand. The sum of one Mark was collected from each

The cover of the programme for the prisoners' Christmas concert at Mensfelden.

The first part of the programme. At No. 12 on the bill, the two Rangers men, Alfred Hall and Arthur Lapworth, join together to render the former's 'favourite song', Afton Water *(words by Robert Burns).*

PROGRAMME OF CHRISTMAS CONCERT 1916

· MENSFELDEN ·

Part 1

1. Jambe de bois — M. Droux.
2. My Wife won't let me — W. Bullworthy.
3. La Bataille de Waterloo — H. Fanlin.
4. Tipperary — H. Clarke.
5. Vive L'Armée — C. Gillig.
6. The Four Komiks present their screaming absurdity :–
   Beer & Skittles
   The Barman — W. Bullworthy.
   Algy Fitzmaurice — E. Booth.
   The Arm of the Law — H. Clarke
   Bruiser Bill — H. Allen
   Scene: Bar Parlour of the Pig & Whistle.

7. Gamin de Paris — M. Briquet
8. Street Watchmans Story — A. Lapworth.
9. Le Vieux Loup de Mer — A. Dube.
10. I'm one of the Boys. — E. Booth.
11. Les Lilas — M. Thomas.
12. Afton Water — { A. Lapworth
                     { A. Hall
13. Le Carllarmeur — M. Péan
14. My Yiddisher Boy — H. Allen.
15. Ma Petite Française — Placide Meur
16. A Broken Window — L. Drummer.
17. Accordeon Solo — M. Bailleul

INTERVAL.

man, French and English, resulting in a total of 37 Marks, carefully accounted in Alfred Hall's notebook. He also listed therein a number of theatrical 'props' which were going to be needed for the planned entertainment:

2 Jews Noses
1 Pair Sideboards (Red)
Grease Paints
Monocle
1 Girls Wig (Red)
1 Whistle
1 Pistol & Caps
1 Moustache
1 Beard
1 Mans Wig
4 pcs Paper

The result of it all was a joint Franco-British production which could rival any West End show – in length at any rate!

January 1st 1916 [sic] *12.15 am*
H.J.C. and I salute the Kaiser Bonne Année.
January 12th 1917
A very severe winter has now commenced, snow falling in considerable quantity all day and night.
The most important question of the hour is: Is it peace or war, and at what terms. I shall willingly stop as a P.O.W. providing the Old Country comes out on top.

January 13th 1917
No news.

January 14th 1917
From 1st Jan we P.O.W. are to be paid in metal money instead of paper checkmarks. What's in the wind. I receive my first payment today. It's nice to feel money again even if does bear the head of Billy K.

The weather then became responsible for a short interlude, the incongruity of which, in their situation, was equalled by its character of light and welcome relief from their harsh lot:

January 17th 1917
The weather has a very cold heart just now, and cold feet, red and streaming noses are very conspicuous. The snow is about 8" deep and being in a frozen state the people here have taken to tobogganing. We, being P.O.W. could only look upon them with envy but, the snow lasting, our envy could not. So, taking the matter into our

An example of the paper money issued to POWs. It would seem, in fact, that it was not entirely superseded by metal money.

own hands and being quite ready to answer for the consequences, we begged and stole sledges and tobogganed to our hearts content. This being our first attempt at tobogganing many of us endeavoured to break down walls, telegraph posts, etc. Our journey took us down a steep hill and we attained a most glorious speed. The inhabitants were astounded at our audacity but eventually came to their usual conclusion that all Englishmen were mad. We arrived at the Barrack late of course and received a sound rating but soft soap and humble pie were effectual. Here endeth the most enjoyable day I've had for nearly two years.

Well, whatever the frustrations of captivity, there were sometimes compensations! Yet, frustration soon regains the upper hand:

February 5th 1917

Were I to put my thoughts on paper they would not make very cheerful reading so leaving myself unwritten for a time I must refer to the news in that 'Intelligent' Rag the 'Frankfurter Nachrichtung', wherein it is stated that President Wilson 'drops his mask' and is on the point of declaring war on Germany. By this time tomorrow I hope it is an accomplished fact. Another interesting fact is that Lloyd George has had an attempt made upon his life by poisoning by 3 women and one man. The hatred against England at the present time is intense and if looks could kill we small band of 15 would have been annihilated many times over. However, we're still here to tell the tale. Never can be imagined a more jealous race of people than these.

Whatever the *Frankfurter Nachrichtung* thought, two more months were in fact to pass before, on 6 April 1917, the United States, having finally abandoned its pacific aspirations, declared war on the Central Powers.

March 3rd 1917
The food question in Germany at the present time is more important than the submarine question. Farmers are of course better off than those unfortunate people in the towns, although the Govt. has now decided to cut down the farmers' domestic necessities.

A man and a woman entered this village today; they had come from a small town (probably Limburg) not far distant. The man was about 5' 10", broad, clean and respectably dressed and about 35 years, the woman about 5' 9", in blue costume, etc, etc. They went from farm to farm begging for bread. I can hardly say 'begging' as he offered to pay for anything they could give him. This was his story: He has just come from Russia (where he had been in the trenches for nearly 2 years) on furlough and on his arrival home had found his wife and children almost starving and altho' he had a little money he was unable to purchase anything for them. (He came to the wrong place when he came to Mensfelden). The people here gave him no bread but on him pleading for a little corn some very grudgingly gave it. And yet these poor misguided people still say 'we shall win'. Because they would be punished if they said otherwise.

In the Middle East, British troops under Sir Stanley Maude had been steadily pushing the Turks back up the valley of the Tigris. On 11 March they entered Baghdad. In Russia, on 8 March, riots had broken out in Petrograd, on 15 March the Tsar abdicated his throne and the sequence of events had begun which were to culminate in the Bolshevik revolution. In France, the German army pulled back several miles to prepared fortified positions known as the 'Hindenburg Line':

March 17th 1917
Fall of Baghdad.
Hurrah!!!!!

Tuesday, March 20th 1917
Revolution in Russia. Petrograd is now a city of blood. Sir George Buchanan is murdered. The Zar is a prisoner and a lot more (I quote German papers). German retirement in France. They gave the ground (including Bapaume, Peronne, etc) up quite voluntary. Their generosity knows no bounds. This is labelled here as 'Hindenburg's strategic move'. Still the people here swallow anything that's thrown at 'em.

Snow again today! Parcels very scarce. No cigarettes. Very little food left in the box. Come, Friede, come.

Sir George Buchanan was the British Ambassador to Russia. The report of his death was an error. He survived to return to Great Britain and die peacefully some years later.

March 21st 1917
Snow again today.
Russia's revolution is still going strong, so is 'Hindenburg's strategic move'.

April 11th 1917
Snow, blizzard and sowing. What a hope!!

April 15th 1917
News comes that I am soon to become an uncle. I am overjoyed at the prospect, yet I did not know that I am fond of infants. (Entry in the barrack of Schoolteacher's kid who walks about whenever he sees Allen with his arms protecting his ears, as Allen told him one day he would cut his ears off). Big battle by Arras. I wish we <u>could</u> shift them back.
    Nothing is more revolting to me than helping these people to sow their grain. That is what makes our position so hard to bear, working against our own nation. This feeling is so overpowering at times that I have great difficulty in keeping from shouting and running amok. Oh! It's <u>awful</u>.

April 23rd 1917
I visit the doctor with skin disease and he orders me back to the Camp. I welcome the change. Our worthy friends (Lieber and family) are making an application for me to stop here in Mensfelden until they (and I, of course) have finished sowing potatoes. I must endeavour to frustrate this pleasant scheme. Hang the blessed spuds. My health must come first.
April 23rd 1917 (continued)
Herr Doctor shares the general hatred against Englishmen. He said today they are all too cheeky and proud, and goodness alone knows what he would do with them if he had his way etc etc etc.

Following the above, there is once more a long gap of over two months, with no entries covering any of his time at Giessen. This might well have been because the keeping of a diary, nominally illegal, was more difficult under the more strictly controlled conditions existing in a camp such as Giessen.

The following entry in Clarke's diary infers that he, too, returned temporarily to Giessen at about this time. Prisoners, such as those he describes, were sometimes sent to work, not only in the German homeland, but also behind the lines, back in the war zone:

May 13th 1917
Today there returned to Giessen from behind the German lines 260 Frenchmen who had been working on road-making, etc. May I never behold again such specimens of humanity. With hollow eyes and sunken cheeks, their clothes hanging on them like sacks, torn and filthy, starved into semi-insanity, they rushed the guards, broke through the barbed wires and ran to us for food.
    That which we gave them although hard as iron, disappeared rapidly. It was of course impossible to feed all, the last comers ran to the waste tubs and scrambled for the refuse.

580 men left Giessen on January 14th 1917 for work behind the German lines, 260 returned, of the remainder 192 died of starvation and brutality or were shot in cold blood, 128 were admitted to hospital on their return to camp, since when many have died. To the civilised mind these facts may seem a trifle exaggerated, but, knowing the Germans as I do, I know it to be true. For instance one party of Frenchmen were returning to their miserable filthy and wet hut in the evening after hard work and no food, when one of them fell down from sheer exhaustion. He made repeated endeavours to keep up with his comrades but at last he fell and could not rise. One of the guards kicked him and hit him with his rifle, whereupon this Frenchman endeavoured to point out that he could not walk. Without more ado the Hun shot him through the head where he lay. The next morning his comrades saw his dried blood but the body had been taken away.

On 28 May 1917, during Hall's sojourn at Giessen, three of his fellow-prisoners at Mensfelden, Sgt Alfred Tong of the Buffs, referred to previously, Sgt Gaythorne Armitage and a Canadian, James Baker, attempted to escape. After some days 'on the run', they were recaptured, but Tong was able to send a letter to his old friends, recounting his adventures, which H.J. Clarke reproduced in his own diary (in several places, Sgt Tong is also constrained to use the Morse Code instead of plain language, presumably out of a sense of propriety. Those of a sensitive nature might prefer to leave these undeciphered):

Arthur Lapworth, in January 1917. On the reverse of this photograph have been written the two poignant words 'In exile'.

Very sorry to tell you we were caught, but all owing to bad luck, for it was a mere accident that it happened, and I will tell you first to last. After we got out of the barrack we turned sharp to the right and went over the little bit of a fence leading into the meadow that you know of course, we went and got our ruck-sacks and different stuff, you know what I got together and I guess I had about 1/2 cwt of stuff in mine, we shared next day. Then we turned into the meadow and went out around Spillmans place and up by the Churchyard and down across the fields into that one of yours that leads into DIEZ way as they call it, that stick half maize and half oats, well we followed that road until just before we reached DIEZ, then turned off into the fields, left DIEZ on our right, we then went across country to the Lahn. We had great difficulty in crossing but now I know every-thing it would be very easy. There are several stone quarries there and a few small boats, but we crossed the first railway bridge out of DIEZ, it was getting daylight so we had to do something a bit quick, we got halfway or hardly so far when a sentry came out of a little house or hut place and told us in German that we were a bit lively this morning, he must have thought we were going somewhere to work. At first we answered ja and then put a little longer face on then he must have been a trifle suspicious for we could hear him letting rip at something for about 5 minutes after we got by. Anyway as soon as we were over the bridge we dived into some thick undergrowth that led out into the corn and then we kept going until we left the Lahn and its sentries a few miles behind. By the way Baker forgot one of his parts of the business, he forgot the water-bottle. Good God, we paid dearly for his forgetfulness, for we had to drink out of the Lahn and I never tasted worse water in my life. I often think of the LIMBURG and DIEZ (... .... .. −) and (.−. .. ..) I must have drunk. Well we must have done about 20 kilometres that is as the crow flies I expect. We anchored in a wood almost too thick to walk into and had a sleep, we were not hungry but a bit tired and wringing with sweat. We slept for a bit but I soon woke up freezing so I pulled out my big knife and cut a lot of branches off the small fir trees and made a damn good bed which we all 3 soon got into and slept until about 1 o'clock then we had a biscuit and a half each and a tin of ham loaf between us and it even filled us up for we did not want any more. We had a small piece of chocolate before we started off at night, that was all that day. We were very thirsty having no water so the first stream we came to we had a good drink but that was all leaves for it was nearly dried up. We done a good night's travelling that night but about 1 or 2 o'clock Baker became sick and kept (... .−. . .− .. −. −.) but we kept going ahead, me with the compass and Gay with Baker just behind lending him a bit of a hand, well towards the finish Baker could hardly travel so I took his pack, that made me a trifle heavy but Gay gave me a spell later on so between us we helped Baker along and got to some shelter where we laid up for the day, that was in some fir trees again but not much good for cover the trees being in rows. I cut some more branches and stuck them in the ground so as no one could see between the rows, during the day a couple of women came within 10 yards of us cutting off dry grass (for bedding I expect) so you can imagine us standing in the rows as tight as we could, eventually they went away at last and we heaved a sigh of relief. Just as we were going away at night a gun was fired just behind us and we heard a dog smelling around and afterwards shake himself but he never came near us, it must have been a gamekeeper. We started off later and went to the main road which we stuck to,

This comradely group has written its own caption. Arthur Lapworth is standing second from the left, Alfred Hall is at the far right, while 'Nobby' Clarke is seated in front of him.

walking along the grass, Baker this night much better which was a great relief to us for the night before he laid down and told us to leave him there and go by ourselves. This night we did not march so far for we did not want to play ourselves out and we expected to be just off the Rhine before morning but not have time to cross it so waited until next night, during that day we suffered terribly from thirst and it rained nearly all day for it was stormy and we were sucking the rain off oak leaves. That day I made an oar for the boat out of a big branch of a tree with three prongs on the end, in these three prongs I weaved brambles just like basket work but they were never used for we went through a big town the next night VALLANDORF and therefore could not take them with us. Well we were in the RHINE valley and that was the only entrance, for there are large cliffs along side, then the road, then the railway, then the RHINE. Well we had to go about something that we did not want to do, either through towns along the RHINE or

Apparently a coffee and card party for five French prisoners and the farmer.

chance the railway which runs along the side of the road, for if we got a boat there is an island in the middle of the river and we should have to cross it twice, so we boarded a goods train which we found was taking iron to DOREIN, 25 K off the Holland frontier. Well we all three laid in the waggon and were having a fine ride after so much walking and were just smiling over our luck when in a station someone was doing something upon one of the trucks, fitting a sailcloth straight over the waggon or something when he happened to glance in and see us and before we had a chance to do anything they had the truck surrounded with railwaymen. They were very much afraid of us for I could hear them outside arguing as to how they could get us out without running any risks to themselves. At last they let the flap down on the platform side and the station-master put his head in and shouted rouse and quickly pulled it out again so we thought it was not much good for there were about 14 I counted, so we came out and stood on the platform until a couple of square-heads came from the town and took us back and put us in cells. We were there 56 hours without a piece of bread and water and I think we were out twice for a (.–. .. ..). I might tell you that we each got a dig under the ear from a big German Pole who thought we were Russians, but after apologised, finding out we were English. There were 95 English about there but never saw any of them, they get up at 1/2 past 4 in the morning, work about $\frac{1}{4}$ past 5 and come home from 12 – 1 for dinner and home again at $\frac{1}{2}$ past 6 at night. Worse than Russians and a damn sight dirtier according to Gay's report as he saw them. Well (–... .–. .– –.–) they let out for a wash just before we came away and we could hardly stand and I could not see anything for *about 10 minutes, everything was yellow, we also got terribly searched, they cut out the lining of my jacket and found all my money and also found Gay's, Baker having none. Gay had 115 Marks, I 113 Marks 35 PFs and they tell us we see that no more for they confiscate all the prisoners' money if he escapes but we are having a good kick to get it. Well we had no food or drink until we got to Limburg and we were there 9 days without bed or basins or anything and had to get in the best barrack we could at night time with the Russians like a lot of sheep drove into pen, and at day they wanted us to work from 7 to 7 at night, with an hour for dinner under a sentry. We got caught the first day but not the second for we never went on parade we hid up all day and had a good sleep but next day morning they had a roll-call we were there but cleared out off the parade before they had a chance to grab us. They tried in the afternoon of the next day and ran us up, we made a complaint to the commandant but he said we must work because we were runaways, then we refused to work but did not crime us with that, just simply sent for the Capt and crimed us for absent off parade a few days before and we got 3 days cells each, that was better than in the barrack for we had a piece of bread and a basin to get water in, that's more than we got outside. Well when we got out the sentry was waiting for us and they were damned glad to see the arse of us. There were funerals every day in Limburg of starving Russians. I am having a fine time here now, me and Gay mess together. Baker has joined his old school. Please give my best to Nobby and Arthur (in particular). You and him (Nobby) done us a damn good turn and thanks to you two <u>Britishers</u> we had a bit of a run for our money which I am afraid we should not have had if not for you two, my hand was numbed for hours after getting it pinched there in that window. Tell Nobby I have been talking to old Crabb, he is also not receiving many parcels but advises him to stop where he is if he has anything of a show at all, for it is a bit of a warm one here for men who are not invalids.*

Not long after the three evaders found themselves once more being marched in through the gates of Giessen, Alfred Hall was taking the opposite route, to return to his familiar life at Mensfelden, still watching the war and with no more taste for the life of a farm labourer than before:

July 1st 1917
I returned from Giessen yesterday, where considering circumstances I had a good time. Now I must look forward to work work work.

I write today to Miss A Lakin regarding the sack of clothing which hasn't come. I also write to Mother asking her to confirm my PC. I have just caught sight of the latest German newspaper and these words struck me as rather comical 'Mit Gott und Hindenburg'. Evidently Billy K has been made to move from the right hand of God to the left to make room for 'Hindy'.

Sunday July 15th 1917
The Frenchman Maurice has been in the cell for 8 days and the rest of his countrymen have decided not to work until he is released, which decision they have passed on to HM the Gefreiter. A deputation of Frenchmen has just gone to the B Meister.

The second of these two groups, having dressed up in silly costumes, looks altogether happier with its lot than the first, which seems to be looking out into a captive future whose length they cannot measure.

Monday July 16th 1917
Maurice released and sent to Wetzlar S C.

July 18th 1917
Lest we forget! The brutal uncivilised treatment of British POW Logan MacDonald,
etc etc etc.
Humour!! The Big Irishman, the German and the Frenchman, the fight for possession!

Sometimes, the entries *are* a bit on the cryptic side!

July 21st 1917
Grace is a muvver, Mater's a grandma, I'm a noncle and Peg's a naunt. Oh ye gods
how old we're getting.

Well, actually he's still only twenty-six, but when you're young and have been incarcerated against your will for over two years, with no apparent sign of an ending, the helpless inner frustration, as days and months of your life are stolen, never to be restored, cannot be denied its expression.

Sunday, July 22nd 1917
Sunday the day of rest! Glorious weather and no freedom yet. Rumours of peace,
exchange of prisoners, etc, etc fill the air. Now for my Sunday's dinner, a few spuds,
piece of horrible meat about the size of my thumb and sauerkraut. And yet I am 'very
lucky'. Connie's letter announcing the river excursion makes my day-dreams turn to
river scenes innumerable. Beautiful scenery, the water, white dresses of some soft clinging
material and FREEDOM. (My hand shakes as I write the word). In fact I nearly
upset the boat on one occasion. Russians retire in Galicia. Fools can't they hold a line.

But it was not to be peace, still less freedom; he was about to experience the most testing months of his long captivity. Two years after his arrival at Mensfelden, the lid over the simmering pot containing Farmer Lieber and himself finally blew off.

CHAPTER 5
Strafe Kommando

In Flanders, the war had evolved: Kitchener's New Armies had become a reality, their ranks swollen further by the introduction of conscription; ever-heavier weights of high explosive were being hurled across the battlefield by the artillery of both sides; the trenches were now complex and semi-permanent systems, while above them in War's new third dimension many more aeroplanes were to be seen, routinely engaging in machine-gun duels, often deadly and adding their contribution to the swelling list of the dead. The Battle of the Somme, with its heavy bill of blood on both sides, had come and gone. In the following June the Third Battle of Ypres had opened, announced by the explosion of huge mines under the German positions on the Messines Ridge. After some initial success for the British, it developed into the slogging fight known as the Battle of Passchendaele, which finally petered out in the mud of a wet autumn, having cost a quarter of a million British casualties. While more rows of crosses sprang up to mark the carnage on both sides of the slaughter line, Alfred Hall could bless his stars that, onerous and unnatural though his life was, he had survived his own small part in the twentieth century's Armageddon. Even so, in that which he was about to experience, he was to find that Death, the fell confederate of War, would renew its appearance, warning that it could strike in places other than the battlefield.

In the normal work *Kommandos* in Germany, such as the one at Mensfelden, the work was hard, the hours long and food short, but life was bearable and even, within the constraints of captivity, occasionally pleasurable. In this, they differed greatly from the *Strafe Kommandos*, or punishment units, to which prisoners were sent who were deemed by the military authorities to have committed some offence. It was to one of these that my father was now consigned, for an unknown period and, needless to say, with no right of appeal.

August 12th 1917
Sunday
Strafe Commando Wetzlar
On July 27th I and L had a tumble in which he fell over a bundle. He accused me of striking him. I spend 8 days in cells, 3 days on bread and water and no bed. I was allowed a warm dinner on the 4th day. Arthur proves himself a real chum and cooks me some good food. I thought cells were bad enough but this place is Hell. Arrived here Saturday Aug. 5th. It is an ironworks. Commenced work Sunday morning 4.30 am finished half dead 9.30 pm. Have now completed 1 week. The food is putrid. Treatment unhuman and terribly hard work being driven like niggers from morning till night. I append our day's routine.

Reveillé 4.30 am. Work 5 o'clock. Breakfast 8.30 to 9 o/c (1 Cup Coffee? no sugar or milk and 1 slice of bread). Dinner 12 o/c to 1 o/c. Swedes and Mangelwurzel soup. Coffee again 3.30 to 4 o/c (same as breakfast). Supper anytime (same as dinner). Have received no parcels and am on the high road to starvation. Cheers.

Wetzlar lies back up the Lahn valley, just a few miles downstream from Giessen and its camp. The ironworks to which he had been assigned was owned by a company called Buderus, which is still in existence. The hours of work would appear to amount to at least 15 each day – surely well in excess of anything envisaged by the Hague Convention. The prisoners' plight was intensified by lack of adequate food. In his predicament, my father penned a couple of letters to his old comrades, appealing for their help. Whether they ever arrived is not known, while the chances of such aid reaching him, locked inside that harsh regime, would have been slim:

Wetzlar Strafe Commando
Friday 15.8.17
Dear Chums
This is the only way that I can see to keep myself and 4 other men here from starvation so I hope you will not think it too great a liberty when I ask you for a parcel of food.

Then, later :

Wetzlar Saturday
I hope you received my previous note. I have been here now 2 weeks. Mac, it's killing. Do try old man and send on one or two parcels for W Rogers (1st Mons) and myself. I'm afraid I must give up all hopes of returning to Mensfelden. I can't write any more just now I'm too damn tired and hungry. With hopes of a speedy reunion in the near future,
I remain
Ever Yr Chum
Alf

As the days pass, exhaustion and lack of nourishment take their toll and the diary, as it sometimes allows him to dwell on memories of happier days, becomes his refuge from a world wholly defined by near-starvation, ill-treatment, hard work and disease. Perhaps not surprisingly, his grip on either the date or the passage of time seems to have become uncertain for a while:

August 18th 1917
Wetzlar
5 weeks of Hell have passed and I am so tired yet I must endeavour to write. What can be the end of such cruelty. Heane dropped out yesterday from sheer exhaustion and they buried him this morning. Perkins is very weak. I wish he would make an effort.

My mind is wandering a bit back to the green fields of old England and Suffolk. Oh, my darling please forgive me. The end doesn't seem far off so perhaps it is all for the best. I see our meadow and those happy days. It is time for the guards to come. There is no rest.

August 20th 1917
Still holding on but very weak. Perkins and 5 Russians were buried yesterday. Rogers and I the only Englishmen left. Do you remember the race to the farm and the glass of milk. Rogers is lying on some clinker. He seems bad I must go to him.

August 21st 1917
Feel a bit better today. They put fat in the soup yesterday. Rogers is still weak but sticking it. 2 Frenchmen carted away. What cattle we are.

Thank you darling for your great love. I have proved so unworthy of it. Can I hold on. I must.

The next few entries are desultory and undated:

A party of British NCOs photographed at Aachen, en route for Holland and home, to be exchanged for a similar party of German prisoners.

My dear dear Mother

Rogers taken to hospital. Some spark of humanity left in these swines.

I have 4 more days here.

Epidemic abating. There seems some hope.

Wednesday, August 29th 1917
(at Dillenburg)
I leave Wetzlar thank God for unknown destination.
    Sitting on the Railway Station at Dillenburg in Westphalia I go over the events of the past few weeks. I can only be thankful that they are finished with and although at present the future is unknown yet it could not be worse than the Strafe Commando at Wetzlar. There are 9 of us here 7 Frenchmen and 2 Englishmen W J Rogers (1st Mons) and myself and the question of the moment is 'Where and what are we bound for'.
    Is it an Iron mine, Coal mine, Iron works or Farm? The latter I think not as Westphalia is the Black Country of Germany. We must 'wait and see'.
    Another interesting topic is the exchange of prisoners. At least I should say the persistent rumours concerning this. I hope it is true, altho' I have long ago given up putting any faith in rumours. My next entry in this book will no doubt be at our mysterious destination.

The same day. 29.8.17
Have arrived! It is an iron mine. Quite a small affair to look at from the top. I haven't been down yet but tomorrow morning at 6 o/c I — descend. We detrained at Neunkirchen (Westf). With our loads we tramped to the World's End at least it seemed so to me — a place in the middle of the forest and there we saw the shaft, the stack and everything there was to see, including a dirty filthy barrack without ventilation and a few dirty filthy Russians. A few minutes of inspection by the sentry in charge and we were allowed to see the interior of our future 'home'. God help us in such a pigstye. They had no dinner for us so gave us some bread and 'coffee'? with a promise of soup at 7 o/c pm, which soup is comprised of the regulation swedes and undergrowth of some description with no meat. The Russians here are an ill looking lot and I can only hope there is truth in the exchange rumour and that it will be realized before I get in such a state. Next entry after I have been down.

So he survived Wetzlar and its deadly diseases, but seemed to have become trapped in the *Strafe Kommando* circuit. By now, conditions at Mensfelden would have seemed rosy by comparison. What were his chances of release from the trap? Was there any truth in the stories of prisoner exchanges?

In July 1917, delegations from both sides of the conflict met at The Hague, to discuss the treatment of prisoners and the exchange of certain categories. The agreements which were reached limited the latter to civilians and service personnel who were medically unfit for combat, so any hopes of exchange my father nursed were almost certainly baseless, particularly in his current status, which seems to have been in danger of diminishing to that of a 'non-person'.

His new home, the iron mine on the Pfannenberg near Neunkirchen, had been open for some fifty years. When it finally closed in 1962, it was reputed to be, at 1,320 metres, the deepest mine in Europe.

Friday, September 7th 1917
Have been down ($\frac{1}{2}$ mile). Am in a poor way, hard work, influenza cold, scanty food, wet feet every day and little sleep. <u>BUT</u> cheers, Red parcels will soon come, perhaps exchange.

Sunday, September 9th 1917
My first experience in a mine was not very exciting although it may have been interesting under different circumstances. On Monday last we turned out of the Barrack at 6 o/c am and went in a room where the overseer told off the new prisoners to their respective places. I (No 32) was ordered to work with a civilian, one Friedman Stahl. This rigmarole finished we adjourned to the pithead and took an acetylene lamp each and then went down under, 4 men in the cage at one time. Arrived at the bottom we found it to be very wet indeed, the water dripping from the roof and at first was very uncomfortable. Stahl and I had to walk about 1 kilometer to the other cage where I discovered we had to descend another 100 yards or so to the new seam. Walking along a distance of 200 yards we reached our destination, except that we climbed up another 30 yards by means of ladders and there commenced work, which consisted of boring, blasting and breaking ironstone and throwing same down a shoot to the landing below where it is loaded on small wagons and taken to the cage and sent aloft. The atmosphere is very close and damp and of course unhealthy and I was glad when 2 o/c pm came and I was able to go aloft in the fresh air. It is strange that I was not affected in any way neither did this my first experience interest me at all. I can only put it down to the fact that being so long bullied and ordered about I take every situation with absolute indifference. The mangels soup and small ration of bread still continues. We are all looking very thin and white. I'd give a small fortune for a tin of bully. It's horrible to feel so hungry. However with a little luck some of us will have our Xmas dinner under more cheerful circumstances.

Still hoping! Nevertheless, never one to waste his time, my father had been putting his detention amidst men of other tongues to good use, in this case the furtherance of his own linguistic education. Thus, he was able to report in his diary the following episode, which provided, for a short while at least, relief from the heavy manual labour which he was forced to accept as his daily lot. It might also be thought to reveal an interesting example of the extraordinarily strict discipline under which even the civilian population in Germany existed:

A contemporary view of Neunkirchen. The cross marks the location of the mine concerned, on the hill known as the Pfannenberg.

The pit-head buildings of the Pfannenberg mine in 1917.

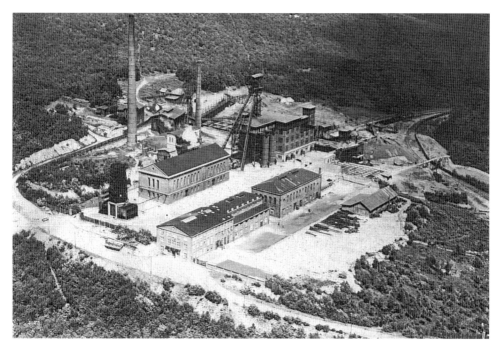

An aerial view of the Pfannenberg mine, taken some years later in 1940. Still at 'the World's End', with dense forest stretching in all directions.

A view of the inside of an ironstone mine dating from that time, this one being at Eiserfeld, just a mile or two to the north of Neunkirchen.

Wednesday 12.9.17
Still another experience!!

It happened that one of the Frenchmen here named Van den Broeck was working on a farm at the Commando of Ruppack. The farm was next to the village school and during his occupation of chopping wood the schoolteacher's wife (age about 40) and daughter (age about 16) passed the time of day to him and had on 2 separate occasions given him cigars. This latter had been seen by 2 or 3 civilians who at once commenced to make mischief with the result that Van den Broeck was sent to the Strafe Commando at Wetzlar for 1 month charged – without trial or hearing – according to prisoners' justice – with intimacy with the ladies above mentioned. This occurred in July 1917. There appears to be some further complications as an order from Frankfurt announced that VdB must go to Siegen together with an interpreter to give a statement. As no Frenchmen here can speak German, I was ordered to go to Siegen with him. My French is bad and my German worse but it was not a difficult ordeal and the magistrate was satisfied so all's well that ends well. The starving appearance of the population of the small town of Siegen is very marked and one cannot help but have pity for the poor kids.

Friday, September 14th 1917
The photograph of mother and baby Roy arrives. It is splendid of the Mater and 'l'enfant terrible' looks very peaceful.

'Mother' is my father's eldest sister Grace. Two more boys, Alan and Colin, arrived after the war, but Roy himself was destined not to survive childhood.

Tuesday, September 18th 1917
Money received from home. For 65/- I receive Mks 103-25. What a drop in the exchange. Am again on the sick list. Last Friday morning managed to get a piece of ironstone in my eye. Went to doctors Saturday. He was away. Went again Sunday morning. He enjoyed himself at my expense with the result that I am blind in the left eye for the next 10 days or so. Anyway it's a rest.

The all important question – when are the parcels coming. Can get no war news in this solitary hole except that the Russians are retiring helter-skelter. It is very lonely here for we two Englishmen and when he is on afternoon shift I am nearly always on mornings.

Sunday, September 30th 1917
Parcels arrived last Wednesday. A feed followed. I feel better in mind, body and estate.

Tuesday, October 2nd 1917
I journey to Giessen to give my statement of the affair at Mensfelden and incidentally read Lieber's statement. He accuses me of intentions to slaughter him, at least, one would gather as much from his statement. It is rather strange that I have been called upon to give my evidence after I have received my punishment. I believe there

is somebody working on my behalf behind the scenes and can make vague guesses who it is.

Wednesday, October 3rd 1917
I return to Neunkirchen.

Saturday, October 27th 1917
I add to my scars by wounding myself over the left eye with a crowbar in my endeavour to help the Germans make shells to kill my own countrymen. Were men ever placed in a more exasperating position. If I had any brains I'd feel inclined to blow 'em out.

Two more weary months then passed, unmarked by any entries in the diary until, as the third Christmas in captivity approaches, the record is resumed:

Sunday, December 16th 1917
It is rather droll to see the Frenchman (François) and the Russian André arguing on the war. François is in favour of war till 'les Boches sont battus' and the Russky is in favour of peace at any price. They both argue in broken German interspersed with their own tongues. Well done François.

Monday, December 17th 1917
The old sentry has just gone. He was the whitest German I've known and my best of good wishes for Xmas and the New Year go with him. The poor old chap nearly cried when he left although he was with us for only 6 weeks.

So a more benevolent attitude towards the German nation is beginning to surface, despite his unhappy experiences, which, compared to the Wetzlar days and although still harsh, seem now to have improved somewhat – if only temporarily – with the arrival of food parcels, letters and books:

December 21st 1917
I am reading 'Griffiths Gaunt' by Chas Reade. This author, to use a phrase of modern civilisation, seems to be 'pulling the public's legs'.

January 10th 1917 [sic]
Some books I must read.
Tom Sawyer by M. Twain II Vol.
Rupert Hentzau by Anthony Hope.
Rolf Boldrewood's works.

I have written to the Camp Commandant for a change or to be sent to the Camp on the plea of ill-health. Without being pessimistic, I do not expect a favourable reply. On Sunday I am writing for more book-keeping books and a book on Commercial Geography. Am still a miner, but it's a horrible life.

Tuesday, February 19th 1918
At 6.30 am Billy Rogers returns to the Camp, having been ill for 4 days caused through the fumes in the mine. This leaves me here alone − alone as far as company is concerned − for my companions at present are 10 Frenchmen 10 Italians and 17 Russians. If I 'beat it' I wouldn't get any farther than 20 kilometers owing to this beastly knee of mine. If I stay here I shall die of melancholia. I must get out of it somehow though.

Wednesday, February 20th 1918
Food very scarce, no parcels!
An inventory of my stock of provisions at present would show:

1 pot Marmite
200 grms Black Bread
150 do. Swiss do.
1 Rasher Bacon
and 3 Haricot Beans
A heap of swede peelings are outside, which I have carefully made a note of, in case of future needs.

Saturday, March 16th 1918
I am returned to Camp.

Wednesday, April 10th 1918
I enter hospital with Bronchitis.
German papers report another 6000 prisoners at La Bassée.
Sorry! it's not Bronchitis. Have just discovered it's inflammation of the throat.

On 21 March had begun the great German offensive which threw the British back many miles in disarray and, for a while, saw the Allies' cause in the greatest peril since the retreat of 1914. More furious assaults were to follow through the summer with heavy casualties on both sides, but in the end the demands on the German war machine proved too great for it to sustain and from some of the darkest months of the war was to emerge the recovery which, in due time and with the help of the newly-arrived Americans, would end in final victory. Only the vaguest notions of these events will have filtered into the *Strafe Kommandos*.

Monday, April 29th 1918
Am sent to Holzappel, Lorenburg, in a mine again. God help us here.

Sunday, May 6th 1918
I write to Camp Commandant Giessen re my position in hell.

Sunday, May 12th 1918
I return to Mensfelden amid many acclamations.

So his appeal to the Camp Commandant had the desired result and his nine months ordeal was at last over. But the diary, which had been suffering from neglect for some time, was now dead, for he made no further entries. It had served its turn, as a solace and a companion, through seemingly endless days which were sometimes lonely, often harsh and, at one point, nearly devoid of hope.

He had now spent almost exactly three years in the unnatural posture of a man who, together with other untold thousands and though guilty of no crime, had been deprived of his liberty and held against his will in an alien land, amid a hostile people. Another six months were to pass before the Armistice was signed and, to the great relief of himself and all his fellow-captives, the day they had awaited for so long came at last. Much time had passed and many events, both great and small, had taken place. It is perhaps true to say that, in most if not all cases, the prisoners returned home with happier thoughts towards their hosts than when they arrived. In my father's case, this was typified by a friendship which originated in an incident, the date of which is uncertain, but which probably occurred during those last months.

One day, a horse was seen galloping into the village, having evidently escaped its attendant. Once brought to a halt, it was, in due time, joined by a panting Alfred Hall, in whose inexpert charge it was supposed to have been. (He may have been using a technique which he had earlier defined in his diary thus: 'When I see the horses faltering I raise my stick in a threatening manner (the gesture is quite an heroic one) and yell at the refractory animals 'Geester' (this is not the correct spelling but it will do). Sometimes they would do as they ought and at other times would jump half out of the harness with fright; that was when I must have looked dangerous I suppose. On these occasions Lieber would hang on to the plough like grim death and swear').

A small crowd had gathered to watch the excitement and from its midst a voice was heard to observe, in perfect English, 'Now that's what I call a lucky accident'. It was thus that he made the acquaintance of 'Tante Bertha' and through her, of Minna (for Wilhelmine) Schwenk, her god-daughter. Bertha Hehner was one of four sisters, all teachers, and her family was one of some standing in the village (one of its main streets is still today called the Hehnerstrasse). Somewhat coincidentally, and as further evidence of the way in which human activities can disdain and transcend the temporary irruptions of war, she had a brother Otto who, having moved to London in 1871, when he was only nineteen, lived there still, being by then a skilled research chemist and a much-respected member of the British scientific community. Minna Schwenk was fated to be more closely and tragically touched by war: on 18 October 1915 her farmer husband, Karl August, was killed in France; twenty-seven years later, her elder son Wilhelm became one of the countless German soldiers who gave their lives to Hitler's campaigns in Russia. With both the aforementioned ladies my father became friendly, a friendship which was to be maintained by letter for some years after the war, although distance and the more limited possibilities of travel in those days precluded any further meetings, once his captivity had ended. Nevertheless, this story serves to

Minna Schwenk, with her two sons, Wilhelm and Karl.

Minna in the fields, with the two boys, her sister Bertha and two of the prisoners.

Left: Otto Hehner in his later years. Right: Bertha Hehner ('Tante'), in 1920.

show that years of living amongst them had enabled Alfred Hall's original hostility towards Germany and its people to be replaced by more friendly feelings. It may stand as a small example of how personal contact can remove an irrational antipathy between persons originally placed in opposing camps by accident of birth and the dictums of history and geography.

So, unlike the many thousands who lay in the Salient and who lie there still, in the marvellously kept cemeteries which dot it, their names inscribed on the stones, 'row on row', or those many other thousands who, lacking any known grave, are remembered on the walls of the Menin Gate and on the memorial wall at Tyne Cot cemetery – unlike them, he returned home at last. Unlike too, those many fellow-prisoners who did not survive their captivity, but who succumbed, for one reason or another, either in the main camps, or out on the *Strafe Kommandos* and the other ordinary work units such as Mensfelden. Just one of these many was Charles Kelly, of 1st Bn the West Yorkshire Regiment, who was captured in August 1914. After enduring over four years of captivity, he died in the barrack at Mensfelden on 1 November 1918, evidently a victim of the influenza epidemic (*die Grippe*) then just beginning to sweep Europe – and only ten days before the day of liberty. In his diary, H.J. Clarke described his last hours:

Sergeant L.H. Bushnell, 16th Canadian Battalion, photographed at Giessen on 20 March 1918. Described as 'the handyman' of the camp by Alfred Hall, while another prisoner reported that: 'he has shown great fearlessness in his dealings with the Germans. He has been of very great assistance to the British prisoners and especially to those who deserved it and were being ill-treated ... Everyone, whether German or British, who had dealings with Sergeant Bushnell had a great respect for him'.

Pte Kelly, West Yorks, died at Mensfelden on Nov 1st 1918 through a disease called Grippe, buried on Nov 4th. How he suffered only God knows. The last 3 days or so he turned delirious. His last night was bad indeed, in his unconsciousness he gave history from Drake, Wellington, etc, then singing and finally praying. A prisoner from September 1914 how hard to die with peace so near at hand (God willed it so). With good treatment he may have pulled through, doctor too late in turning up. We did our best but that was little for we did not know how to treat him. One Russian and two French have died during the last week in the next village from same disease and several by Limburg.

MONUMENT ERECTED IN MEMORY OF THE
PRISONERS OF WAR WHO DIED IN
CAPTIVITY AT GIESSEN. R. I. P.

*Memorial erected at
Giessen to those who died
while in captivity there.*

Architect: Alb. Depondt.   Sculptor: Raph. Drouard.

*The grave of Private C.P. Kelly, 1st Bn
The West Yorkshire Regiment, who died at
Mensfelden on 1 November 1918 and was
buried there. His remains were later moved
and now lie in the British military cemetery
at Niederzwehren, 10 miles south of
Kassel. The present whereabouts of this
gravestone (which was erected at Mensfelden
by his comrades) are not known.*

109

The graves of Private Kelly and of Rifleman I.G. Moreton (see page 81), in the cemetery at Niederzwehren.

CHAPTER 6

Russian Mission

So at last the Armistice was signed, the guns ceased to speak and the politicians were left to resume their habitual scheming and negotiating. In due course the prisoners of all the combatant nations returned to their far-flung homes, to pick up the threads of normal life once more.

That the First World War was a seminal experience for all who lived through it must be a self-evident truth, though most especially for those who knew the privations of the trenches and the horrors of the open field. My father saw a little of those, although he was spared the later and ultimate excesses of the Somme and Passchendaele. On to his short experiences of battle were added those of the more passive years of captivity – which, while of a different nature from those of the battlefield, nevertheless represented a long theft from the normal human entitlement to liberty, not for any crime, but for serving his country. Did all this have a modifying effect on his personality? Needless to say, I am in no position to compare his character before his experiences with that of his later years. For all that, it must surely be true that, on his return after four years' absence, his family and friends found an Alfred Hall, not just more mature than the young man whom they had last seen shortly before Christmas 1914, but one who had matured considerably more than the four-year interval would normally imply. One is certainly inclined to presume that the unnatural existence to which he and his comrades had been subjected, at such a formative period of their lives, would, to some extent, have shaped certain of their attitudes during the remainder of their days. One would nevertheless also judge that, in his case and in that of the great majority of his comrades, the robust nature of the human spirit will have allowed it all to be assimilated, perhaps with a modification of their characters, but without any deep mental scars.

After his return home, he had to wait until March 1919 before the Army allowed him to resume his civilian status. Several events then took place in rather rapid succession. On the 10th, he was demobilized. On the 15th he and my mother were married and took the train to Ilfracombe for their honeymoon. On the 24th, immediately after their return, my father joined the staff of the British Red Cross Society (BRCS), once more to don a British Army uniform and then to take up duties which, of all things, entailed his immediate return to Germany and its prison camps, which he had so recently and thankfully left.

Although the coming of peace had in general enabled the great armies of POWs held by the combatant nations to return to their own homes, this was not true in the case of one large body of captives who still languished in Germany's *Lagers*. These were the unfortunate Russians, whose immediate release and return had been impeded by the tumult in their native lands where, in the wake of the Revolution,

2844. Pte. Hall. A.W.

BUCKINGHAM PALACE

1918.

The Queen joins me in welcoming you on your release from the miseries & hardships, which you have endured with so much patience & courage.

During these many months of trial, the early rescue of our gallant Officers & Men from the cruelties of their captivity has been uppermost in our thoughts.

We are thankful that this longed for day has arrived, & that back in the old Country you will be able once more to enjoy the happiness of a home & to see good days among those who anxiously look for your return.

George R.I.

The letter from the King which was issued to all returned prisoners of war.

civil war raged and anarchy reigned. Their plight was desperate, for Germany too was in turmoil and teetering on the brink of civil war. The Kaiser had gone to exile in Holland and a republic had been proclaimed, but the country was starving. There was certainly no food to spare for any Russians whom the recent tides of history had left stranded in their midst. As for help from the latters' own nation, that was clearly out of the question.

The gravity of their predicament had been recognised at a very early point after the ending of hostilities. On 8 December 1918, with the Armistice but four weeks old, Edouard Frick, representing the International Committee of the Red Cross (ICRC) in Geneva and accompanied by M. Kassianov of the Russian Red Cross, had visited the British Embassy in Paris and had there submitted a memorandum on the subject. This proposed that the ICRC should set up a chain of 'concentration camps', from the Baltic to the Black Sea, into which the returning Russians would be received, classified, fed and finally helped to regain their homes. In pledging that the ICRC would be responsible for these activities, M. Frick asked that the British and French Governments lend their support in the form of financial aid, to the tune of not less than half a million francs.

This proposal was not sympathetically received by the British Government. At a meeting at the War Office on 31 December, it was concluded that, in the conditions then existing in the former Russian Empire, M. Frick's scheme was 'unworkable'. For one thing, many of the places involved in the ICRC scheme were by then in the hands of the Bolsheviks. Instead, the War Office proposed to take action itself, in Germany rather than in Russia, through an Inter-Allied Control Commission, located in Berlin and headed by Maj.-Gen. Sir Richard Ewart. This Commission was duly established in February 1919, with the objectives of 'providing for the improvement of the material and moral conditions of Russian Prisoners of War in Germany' and 'effecting their eventual repatriation'. (Another of its tasks was the location of British POWs who were still in Germany but who had disappeared and could not be accounted for.)

Although the offer from the ICRC had been turned down, the task was clearly of a nature which placed it, partially at least, within the range of activities habitually undertaken by the Red Cross. The BRCS was therefore invited to take part in the operations. Other organisations, such as the American YMCA, also seem to have been involved. My father, with his recent first-hand experience of German POW camps and his working knowledge of the German language, offered his services and was accepted, becoming an accredited member of the BRCS staff. Thus it was that he found himself, with other colleagues, travelling first to Holland and then to Germany itself. This time, however, the train which bore him eastward would offer somewhat greater comfort than the one in which he had ridden four years earlier and his own circumstances would be vastly more agreeable, although somewhat marred by the fact that, after so short a time with her, he was obliged to leave his new bride behind.

In the confused conditions then pertaining, the total number of Russians involved was unknown, although one source put it at half a million. They were spread among many camps across Germany, of which Celle, Sennelager and Paderborn were only three. With other colleagues, my father spent his time at the two last-named. To assist them in their task, working as they were in a military environment and negotiating with the German authorities still nominally responsible for the camps, they were issued with British officers' uniforms and provided with papers which accorded them the status of lieutenant. The most immediate and urgent of the tasks before them was the supply of food. Fortunately, a large stock of food parcels, which had been intended for British POWs, still lay in Holland. Now no longer required for their original purpose, they could be most usefully employed to meet this surviving emergency. Transfer of these stores to the camps in Germany now began, where the much-needed food was distributed to their Russian inmates, under the supervision

IRL/12 Jan/12562

CERTIFICATE of* { Discharge / Transfer to Reserve / Disembodiment / Demobilization } on Demobilization.

Army Form Z. 21.

N.B.—Any person finding this Certificate is requested to forward it in an unstamped envelope to the Secretary, War Office, London, S.W. 1.

WARNING.—If this Certificate is lost a duplicate cannot be issued. You should therefore on no account part with it or forward it by post when applying for a situation.

Regtl. No. 470667 .... Rank.... Rfm

Names in full.... Hall .... Alfred William
(Surname first)

Unit and Regiment or Corps from which } *Discharged Disembodied / Transferred to Reserve } 12th Bn. London Regt.

Enlisted on the.... 7-9-1914

For.... 10th Bn. London Regt.
(Here state Regiment or Corps to which first appointed)

Also served in.... Nil

Only Regiments or Corps in which the Soldier served since August 4th, 1914, are to be stated. If inapplicable, this space is to be ruled through in ink and initialled.

†Medals and Decorations awarded during present engagement } Nil
authorised prior to 11.11.18

*Has / Has not } served Overseas on Active Service.

Place of Rejoining in case of emergency } Crystal Palace .... Medical Category....

Specialist Military qualifications } Nil .... Year of birth.. 1891

He is* { Discharged / Transferred to Army Reserve / Disembodied / Demobilized } on 10-3-1919
in consequence of Demobilization.

A. Reynolds Cole .... Signature and Rank. Col.

Officer i/c.... Records.... (Place)
INFANTRY RECORD OFFICE LONDON.

* Strike out whichever is inapplicable. † The word "Nil" to be inserted when necessary.

(20936). Wt. W 8211—P.P. 2329. 3,000m. 1/19. D & S. (E 1256.)

Rifleman Hall's Demobilisation Certificate (left) and his army identity document (below), certifying his BRCS credentials.

No. 18910   Name of Holder Hall - Alfred William   No. of Brassard Certificate 18910
Lat Badge B.282.   No. of Passport _____   No. of Brassard (Armlet) 18910

Nationality British

Civil Status Storekeeper

B.R.C.S. - Russian Prisoners of war - Holland

Apparent Age 28

Height 5 ft 7 in

Colour of Hair fair

Colour of Eyes blue

Visible Marks (such as Scars on face, loss of Fingers, &c., &c.) :—
small scar on chin.

Signature of Competent Military Authority :—
James Chagill   Colonel

Signature of Chairman of Joint Committee of The British Red Cross Society and Order of St. John :—

Date and Place of Issue :—
London
24. 3. 19.

Signature of Holder
Alfred W. Hall

114

of the BRCS personnel. Gradually, as the condition of the prisoners improved, it became possible to organise and encourage sports and entertainments, to lift and maintain their morale while arrangements went forward for their repatriation.

Although the relief of the stranded Russians was clearly a humanitarian activity, in the hard-headed world of international politics, inevitably such men also became hapless pawns in a deeper game. British ministers were constrained to find in the situation a political factor, which they believed had to be taken into account. The war between the Bolsheviks and the White Russians was still going on; the British Government hoped, of course, that the latter would win – indeed, it had sent forces to assist them. The fear was expressed that, if the Russian prisoners were returned, they would not only be recruited into the Communist armies, but would also be used by the Bolsheviks for propaganda purposes. Winston Churchill, now at the War Office, made a typically forthright contribution, in a note to the Deputy Chief of the Imperial General Staff and others, on 16 April 1919:

> *Pray meet together today and, after discussion between yourselves, present to me through the CIGS a statement marshalling the grave reasons which exist against the wholesale repatriation to Russia of Russian prisoners of war in Germany.*
>
> *Whereas we could have made out of these an army of loyal men who would have been available to sustain the defence of Archangel and Murmansk or to aid General Denekin and Koltchak, we are now I presume simply sending a reinforcement of 500,000 trained men to join the armies of Lenin and Trotsky. This appears to me to be one of the capital blunders in the history of the world.*

Of course, they were sent back. The prisoners themselves, understandably, if unwisely in some cases, wanted to go home, the German authorities were demanding their repatriation, complaining that some 18,000 of their troops were being diverted to the task of guarding them, while the BRCS, for its part, announced that it would cease operations and withdraw its personnel with effect from 1 August.

So far as Sennelager was concerned, on 15 July the prisoners were placed on board trains, whence they were carried eastwards, bound for what was then called Preussische Holland on the Russo-German border (now the Polish town of Pastek) and an uncertain future in the new Russia. For Alfred Hall, this finally marked the end of his connections with the 'Great War', although the memories of course remained. Together with his colleagues, he returned for a second time to his own country and at last put off the uniform which had been his daily garb for the last five years.

Honorary Lieutenant Hall of the British Red Cross Society.

D a u e r - A u s w e i s .

Der engl. Leutnant Alfred H a l l hat die Erlaub-
nis, sich im Lager frei zu bewegen und nach Paderb.
zu fahren.

Sennelager, den 5. Mai 1919.

Major und Kommandant.

*The Permit (*Dauer-Ausweis*) issued to Leutnant Alfred Hall by the German authorities,
permitting him to enter the camp at Sennelager and also to travel to the nearby camp at
Paderborn.*

Three BRCS officials: Morris, Parsons and Hall, pictured with three Russian officers.

Gilbert Parsons, also of the BRCS. The regimental badges on the BRCS officials' caps were replaced by the standard Red Cross insignia.

Lts Parsons and Hall in the photographer's studio with Russian officers Chowanski, Palschevski and Polonovitch.

Ivan Ivanovitch (in British Army uniform), described as a great helper.

IVAN IN ENGLISH UNIFORM.

Russian POWs lined up for the start of the 200 metres race during the Sports Day held at Sennelager in June 1919. The starter is Piper, of the United States YMCA, and the judges are Hall and Morris, of the BRCS.

During this period, Sennelager camp also fielded a football team. It was made up of players from five nations: Belgium, Great Britain, France, Germany and Russia (including, inevitably, Lt Hall, seventh from the right).

The band formed by the Russian POWs at Sennelager, photographed on 26 June 1919. Seated, from left to right: Tylor, Hall, Morris, Russian interpreter.

The menu of the farewell dinner at Sennelager before the diners went their separate ways.

A u s w e i s .

Die von dem Britischen Roten Kreuz Leutnant

A. W. H a l l mitgeführten Gepäckstücke sind geprüft,

und enthalten nur persönliches Eigentum und Lebensmittel

des Britischen Roten Kreuzes.

Sennelager, den 31. Juli 1919.

Rittm.& st.Kommandant.

The pass issued by the German camp authorities to Alfred Hall, on completion of his duties at Sennelager, certifying that he is carrying only his personal possessions and British Red Cross provisions.

The scene at Sennelager railway station on 15 July 1919, prior to the departure of the former Russian prisoners for their homeland.

The Russians boarding their train in readiness for departure.

Russian officers and British officials see the train off on its journey, bound for Preussische Holland, on the then Russo-German frontier.

Chapter 7

Postscript

On 28 June 1919, the Peace Conference at Versailles came to an end, with the signing of the Peace Treaty which, like that in Vienna just over a century before, redrew the map of Europe, not, it was to be found, altogether successfully.

Ordinary people like my father got on with their lives as well as they could, in a world which probably in many ways seemed a natural continuation of the one they had last seen in 1914, even though later on great changes would, in retrospect, be seen to have taken place. As those two uneasy inter-war decades passed, he gradually resumed his commercial career and settled down to an unexceptional and comfortable married life, in the course of which he raised a family, acquired his first motor car and served his term as President of his local Chamber of Commerce. In his leisure hours, he played a lot of cricket, cultivated his garden and enjoyed his annual fortnight's relaxation by the sea with his wife and two sons, usually either in Suffolk or the West Country, while the passing years pushed his wartime experiences progressively deeper into the well of memory. They nevertheless remained vivid; during those years he could on occasion be drawn to recount some of them, either in the Salient or in captivity. However, once the Second World War had begun, I do not recall him ever referring to them again. Reflecting on this, I have been inclined to conclude that, with the arrival of a new war, he felt that no one would any longer want to listen to an old soldier's tales of his own small part in the earlier one.

Be that as it may, at 11.15 on that Sunday morning of 3 September 1939, he, with the rest of his generation and the new one which had grown up, were to find, via the reedy voice of Neville Chamberlain, that all would seemingly have to be done again. Fortunately, for him at least, he was then old enough to escape a second call to join the fighting in Flanders.

He was, however, destined to have one last brush with the Hun. During that summer of 1940, he was working for an outpost of the War Office in a requisitioned house in Chislehurst, Kent. When, after Dunkirk, Anthony Eden announced the formation of the Local Defence Volunteers (LDV), which became the Home Guard, one of its units which mustered was based on those offices and my father enrolled in its ranks. One day that August, as the air battles raged over the country's southern skies, a German Dornier 17 bomber was apparently spotted, at low altitude. The platoon was turned out and ordered to fire a volley at the intruder, which crashed shortly thereafter. In all probability, the aircraft had previously been mortally damaged by something more lethal than a few rifle bullets and was on its way to earth anyway. Nevertheless, with morale-boosting news hard to come by at the time, the Home Guard was credited with its demise and the platoon enjoyed a brief fame on the front pages of all the national newspapers.

Later on still, some years after that second war had ended, he compiled a selection of his favourite verses, writing them out on sheets of parchment in his immaculate copperplate, which he then bound into a small loose-leaf book, which I still possess. One of those verses, by Walter de la Mare, which contained echoes of that old conflict in which he was a very minor participant, is reproduced here.

Peace

Night is o'er England, and the winds are still:
Jasmine and honeysuckle steep the air;
Softly the stars that are all Europe's fill
Her heaven-wide dark with radiancy fair;
That shadowed moon now waxing in the west
Stirs not a rumour in her tranquil seas;
Mysterious sleep has lulled her heart to rest,
Deep even as theirs beneath her churchyard trees.

Secure, serene; dumb now the night-hawk's threat;
The guns low thunder drumming o'er the tide;
The anguish pulsing in her stricken side........
All is at peace...... But, never, heart, forget:
For this her youngest, best, and bravest died,
These bright dews once were mixed with bloody
Sweat.

'Peace' by Walter de la Mare, transcribed in copperplate by Alfred Hall.

Bibliography

Anon., *Handbook to Belgium and the Battlefields*, Ward, Lock.

Chapman, Paul, *In the Shadow of Hell*, Leo Cooper, 2001.

Edmonds, Brig. J.E., and Wynne, Capt. G.C., *Military Operations, France and Belgium, 1915*, Imperial War Museum/The Battery Press, 1995 (originally published 1927).

McWilliams, J., and Steel, R.J., *Gas! The Battle for Ypres 1915*, Vanwell Publishing, 1985.

Moorehead, Caroline, *Dunant's Dream: War, Switzerland and the History of the Red Cross*, Harper Collins, 1998.

Murphy, Lt-Col. C.C.R., *The History of the Suffolk Regiment 1914-1927*, Hutchinson, 1928.

A Rifleman, *Four Years on the Western Front*, Naval & Military Press (originally published by Odhams, 1922).

Wheeler-Holohan, Capt. A.V,. and Wyatt, Capt. G.M.G., *The Rangers' Historical Records*, Harrison & Sons.

Other Reference Sources

Imperial War Museum:

Misc 30 (544): Account by a Mr Castle of working for the Red Cross in aid of Russian POWs held in German Prison Camps in 1919.

88/57/1: Letters home written by Rfm. B. Britland, 8th Bn The Rifle Brigade, from Ypres and Giessen.

Public Record Office:

FO383/20: Correspondence on POWs.

FO383/151: FO Prisoner of War and Alien Department – General Correspondence from 1906.

HO45/10763/270829: Records of the Committee on the Treatment by the Enemy of British POWs.

HO45/10764/270829: Records of the Committee on the Treatment by the Enemy of British POWs.

T1/12446: Treasury Papers.

WO32/5377: Retention of Military Mission in Germany, 1919.

WO32/5378: Policy regarding repatriation of Russian Prisoners of War in Germany.

WO95/128: The War Diary for 1914-1915 of the 12th County of London Battalion (TF).

WO161/104: The London Territorial Force.

Acknowledgements

I grew up in the shadow of the Great War – in the days when it was that war to which the term 'the Last War', still well-used today, was applied in conversation, until it was superseded by the new one which broke out on 3 September 1939. As a boy, I remember amusing myself looking at my father's collection of wartime photographs, Field Service postcards and other souvenirs of those terrible four years, whilst being too young to comprehend the fearful realities represented by the objects which I held in my hand. I knew all about the Great War of 1914–1918, yet knew very little. I suspect that I echo many sons in wishing that I had taken more trouble in my earlier years to question him about his experiences before it was too late. So, first of all, my thanks are due to him for preserving that collection of papers, notebooks and photos from which I have tried to reconstruct those few aberrant years of his early life.

My elder brother Phil has been invaluable, both as the later guardian of that archive and in being able to contribute a number of anecdotal details: on those occasions before the Second World War when our father could be drawn to recount some of the events of *his* war, it was my brother who was old enough to take an interest, whereas I generally preferred to be playing with my toy soldiers....

Next, my deepest thanks go to my friend of more years than either of us care to remember, Tom Cunningham of Werl, in Nordrhein-Westfalen, for all the enthusiastic help he rendered, from his home conveniently close to the region of Germany where my father had spent his captivity. To him I owe all the additional information we have been able to glean about the different places involved. Most importantly, it was Tom's initiatives which resulted in that very happy day when he, my brother and I enjoyed the warm hospitality of the present members of the Schwenk family and were shown around the modern village of Mensfelden, where our father had lived and worked as a prisoner for three years. Tom's efforts, helped by his wife Toni, ensured that considerably more substance could be given to the account of the events which took place in Germany than would otherwise have been the case.

Tom also, in the course of his researches, discovered Herr Wilhelm Lieber, a local historian, who also earns my thanks for his interest and his great help on the spot.

I should like also to express my warmest thanks to Ian Swindale, for entrusting to me the diary of 'Nobby' Clarke, Mensfelden POW and erstwhile signaller with the 1st Suffolks, and for his permission to include passages from it.

In the same connection, my thanks are also due to the Brotherton Library at Leeds University and to Richard Davies in particular, for first bringing the above diary to my notice and for his good offices in putting me in touch with Ian.

That excellent national institution, the Public Record Office at Kew, has proved invaluable to my research into many of the events concerned and my thanks are due to the staff there. A list of the PRO files consulted and quoted from is given under 'Other Reference Sources', on the preceding page.

I must also express my thanks to staff of the Imperial War Museum. The relevant IWM files, which rendered useful background information, are also listed on the previous page.

The majority of the photographs used in this book are from my father's own collection and a number of the others are in my own possession. The sources of the remainder are as follows:

Pages 17(b), 30(t), 31, 32: The Trustees of the Imperial War Museum.

Pages 98(b), 99(t): Karl Heinz Wildtraut (via Tom Cunningham).

Page 106(t): Elsbeth Will (*née* Schwenk).

Last, but not least, I should like to thank Alan Sutton and Tempus Publishing for bearing with me and my endeavour to place on record this tale in a minor key of how the massive eruption of the Great War treated just a few of the millions of hapless, ordinary people caught up in its events.